JOHN BURTON RACE
FLAVOUR
FIRST

photographs by David Loftus

Quadrille

First published in 2008 by Quadrille Publishing Limited
Alhambra House, 27-31 Charing Cross Road, London WC2H 0LS
www.quadrille.co.uk

This paperback edition published in 2010

Text © 2008 John Burton Race
Photography © 2008 David Loftus
Design and layout © 2008 Quadrille Publishing Limited

Cataloguing in Publication Data: a catalogue record for this book is available from the British Library.

ISBN 978 184400 828 5

Printed in China

Editorial director **Anne Furniss**   Creative director **Helen Lewis**   Project editor **Janet Illsley**
Art direction & design **Vanessa Courtier**   Photographer **David Loftus**   Production **Ruth Deary**

In memory of
Denys Arthur Race

NOTES

• All spoon measures are level unless
otherwise stated: 1 tsp = 5ml spoon;
1 tbsp = 15ml spoon.
• Use sea salt, freshly ground pepper
and fresh herbs unless otherwise
suggested.
• Egg sizes are specified where they
are critical, otherwise use medium
(60g) eggs – ideally organic or at
least free-range.
• Anyone who is pregnant or in a
vulnerable health group should
avoid recipes using raw egg
whites or lightly cooked eggs.
• Timings are for conventional
ovens. If you are using a fan-assisted
oven, reduce the temperature by
10-15°C (½ Gas mark). Use an oven
thermometer to check the accuracy
of your oven settings.

CONTENTS

FOOD is a subject that you never stop learning about, which is probably why I find it so fascinating. When I lived in France, I was able to walk around the local markets and see and taste different ingredients coming into season. Now I'm pleased and proud to witness a growth in the farmers' markets in this country, showing off the very best of our seasonal produce. It makes it so much easier to create a great dish if you start off with fantastic raw ingredients.

I love the idea that you should be able to taste before you buy, as they do in Europe. How often have you been tempted by a fine-looking peach on a supermarket shelf, only to find once you have bought it and bitten into it, that it's hard and acidic? You should be able to feel, smell and, where possible,

taste food so that you know what you are buying. I choose fruits in season and use various methods to preserve them when they are at their best, and I suggest you do the same – you'll find some ideas in the fruit section. It enables you to give more variety to your cooking throughout the year without resorting to imported produce that has been picked before ripening and is lacking in flavour.

Fundamentally, this book is about making the most of ingredients when they are at their freshest, tastiest and cheapest. It is about appreciating fine fresh fish and good quality succulent meat. It is about identifying the best ingredients, buying them in season and transforming them into great-tasting dishes. Fifty per cent of good food is about the raw ingredients. The rest is down to the recipe and skill of whoever happens to be cooking.

Here I've tried to offer the enthusiastic cook a taste of my passion for good food. My favourite ingredients are featured and I give you a choice of dishes to prepare with them. I hope by the time you reach the end of the book, like me, you'll be mad about food!

VEGETABLES

ASPARAGUS

This vegetable is available most of the year round as it is flown in from warmer climes, but my advice is always to buy it when it's in season. Homegrown asparagus has an incomparable flavour – deliciously sweet and juicy, with a slight aniseed aftertaste. The season usually starts in early May, but sadly lasts for only about 6–8 weeks, so make the most of it.

When you are buying asparagus, look for tightly furled tips that aren't moist or discoloured in any way. Also, check the stems are firm and uniformly coloured. To test for freshness, hold a spear between your fingers and snap it – the stalk should break sharply like a stick. The firmer it is, the fresher it is. After buying, keep in the salad drawer of the fridge, wrapped in a slightly damp cloth, for up to 2–3 days.

To prepare the vegetable for cooking, snap off the woody ends, then finely peel the stems to just below the tips, using a swivel vegetable peeler. Bring a pan of well salted water to a rolling boil, add the asparagus spears and cook until al dente (retaining a bite). This will take about 4 minutes, depending on the thickness of the stems. Don't leave them in the water once they are ready – overcooked asparagus is slimy and awful. Remove with tongs and drain carefully. Serve at once or refresh in a bowl of icy cold water.

Asparagus is a wonderfully versatile vegetable. It is delicious hot, simply topped with melting butter and perhaps a sprinkling of chopped chervil and sea salt. It is equally good served warm with hollandaise or mayonnaise, or transformed into a mousse to serve as a decadent starter. I also love to use it in risottos and pasta dishes.

ASPARAGUS RISOTTO WITH PEAS AND BROAD BEANS

I use a chicken stock when I'm making this risotto, because I find it gives more depth of flavour to the finished dish, but you can, of course, use a vegetable stock for a true vegetarian version. Vegetables that are surplus from other dishes can also be added.

300g asparagus spears

salt and pepper

300g freshly podded fresh peas (about 750g weight in the pod)

300g freshly podded broad beans (about 600g weight in the pod)

2 tbsp olive oil

2 shallots, peeled and finely diced

1 garlic clove, peeled and finely crushed

1 litre chicken or vegetable stock (see page 248)

350g risotto rice, such as arborio

125g mascarpone cheese

75g Parmesan, freshly grated

10g mint leaves, finely chopped

50g butter

4 SERVINGS

1 Snap off the tough stalks of the asparagus spears and peel the lower end of the stalks. Bring a large pan of salted water to the boil, add the peas and boil for 4–5 minutes until just tender. Remove with a slotted spoon and refresh under cold running water. Repeat with the broad beans and then the asparagus, cooking the beans for 3–4 minutes and the asparagus for 2–3 minutes only. Set the vegetables aside while you make the risotto.

2 Place a large heavy-based pan over a medium heat and add the olive oil. When hot, add the shallots and garlic and sweat, without colouring, until the shallots are tender and sweet, about 5 minutes. In the meantime, bring the stock to the boil in another pan and keep it at a low simmer.

3 Tip the rice on to the shallots and stir to coat in the oil. Next, add a ladleful of the hot stock and stir frequently until it is absorbed. This helps to release the starch from the rice and makes the risotto creamy. As each ladleful of stock is absorbed, add another. Continue this process until the rice is tender, yet the individual grains remain separate; it will take about 15–20 minutes.

4 Now stir in the blanched vegetables, mascarpone, grated Parmesan, chopped mint and butter. Place a lid on the pan, take off the heat and leave the risotto to rest for 5 minutes before serving.

5 Divide the risotto among warmed bowls and accompany with a crisp salad.

WARM ASPARAGUS MOUSSE WITH A CHERVIL BUTTER SAUCE

These delicious little mousses make a lovely, light starter. I can't think of anything I'd rather eat before a main dish of new season's lamb.

800g asparagus spears

salt and pepper

150g boneless, skinless
   chicken breast

1 whole egg, plus 1 egg
   yolk

4 chervil sprigs, chopped

200ml milk

150ml whipping cream

TO SERVE

1 bunch of baby leeks,
   trimmed and washed

25g butter

300ml warm butter sauce
   (see page 249)

4 tbsp chervil, chopped,
   plus extra sprigs to
   garnish

10g truffle (optional),
   sliced into julienne

6 SERVINGS

1 Preheat the oven to 170°C/Gas 3. Butter 6 ramekins and line the base of each one with a disc of greaseproof paper.

2 Snap off the ends and peel the asparagus spears from just under the tip to the bottom. Cook in a pan of lightly salted boiling water for 4–5 minutes until soft. Drain and refresh in ice-cold water; drain well. Cut the tips (about 3cm) from 18 spears and reserve these for the garnish.

3 Put the chicken, whole egg, egg yolk and chervil in a blender and blitz for 30–40 seconds. Add the asparagus and a pinch each of salt and pepper and whiz until smooth. Next, add the milk and cream and blitz until smooth and velvety. Pass this mixture through a fine sieve into a bowl.

4 Fill the ramekins with the asparagus mousse mixture. Stand them in a roasting tin and surround with hot water to come two-thirds of the way up the sides. Lay another disc of greaseproof paper on top of each mousse. Carefully place in the oven and cook for 25–30 minutes until firm to the touch.

5 Meanwhile, cook the leeks in boiling salted water until just tender. Drain, refresh in iced water, drain and pat dry. Cut into 3cm pieces (the same length as the asparagus tips).

6 Just before serving, melt the butter in a sauté pan and gently reheat the leeks and asparagus tips. Season with salt and pepper to taste.

7 Add the chopped chervil to the butter sauce and warm gently, but don't boil or it will split.

8 When the mousses are ready, remove from the tray and run a knife around each one to loosen. Carefully turn out on to warmed serving plates, arrange the leeks and asparagus alongside and spoon over the chervil sauce. Sprinkle with the truffle (if using) and garnish with chervil. Serve at once.

ASPARAGUS WITH DRY CURED HAM

The first new season's asparagus is one of my favourite ingredients. If you cook it properly the initial taste you get is something a little reminiscent of aniseed, then there's a lovely nutty back flavour before you taste the vegetable. This dish is a very simple one, but the saltiness of the ham complements the sweetness of the asparagus perfectly.

800g asparagus spears
salt and pepper
100ml tarragon
    vinaigrette (see
    page 250)
100g sliced Serrano or
    Parma ham
handful of chervil sprigs,
    to garnish

4 SERVINGS

1   Snap off the bottom of the asparagus stalks and peel them finely from just below the tips to the base. Be careful as they break easily.

2   Bring a pan of salted water to the boil. Add the asparagus and cook for about 4 minutes until just tender. Immediately drain and refresh the asparagus in a bowl of ice-cold water. Drain well and place in a bowl.

3   Shake the dressing to combine, then strain over the asparagus and toss to coat. Season with salt and pepper to taste. Divide the asparagus into 4 bundles.

4   Wrap the bundles loosely in the slices of dry-cured ham and lay on serving plates. Drizzle the remaining dressing around the asparagus and garnish with chervil sprigs. Serve as a light lunch or evening snack, with some good bread.

GLOBE ARTICHOKES

These deserve to be classified as a vegetable delicacy, along with asparagus. They have a distinctive flavour, which is almost nutty and sweet. The vegetable is actually the bud of a large thistle flower and is somewhat fiddly to prepare, but well worth the effort in my view.

Globe artichokes are not widely produced in this country, but those that are homegrown are at their best from June through to November. They are, however, grown abundantly in sun-kissed areas of Europe, particularly in Brittany, Spain and Italy – ranging from the pale green, round variety common in Brittany to the small, elongated purple artichokes found in Tuscany and the south of France. These are tender enough to be eaten whole – even raw dipped into a dressing.

When you are buying artichokes, look for ones with dark green, tightly packed leaves and note that, in the case of this vegetable, big isn't always best. Smaller, young artichokes will be more tender. They are best eaten as fresh as possible, though you can keep them in the salad drawer of the fridge for a few days.

Prepare and cook globe artichokes (as described overleaf), removing all the inedible parts, to leave the succulent hearts. Dip these into a lovely lemon butter sauce or hollandaise, or serve them cold with a herb vinaigrette. Sliced artichokes are also delicious tossed through tagliatelle or used as a topping for pizzas. Or you could sauté some with herbs and serve them as a different accompaniment to meat and fish dishes.

TO PREPARE GLOBE ARTICHOKES

Wash in cold water, then lay the artichoke on its side and cut off the stalk with a sharp knife to expose the base. Now, slice off the top third to remove the tough pointed ends of the leaves. Cut around the artichoke to remove the outer leaves. Rub the cut surface with lemon juice to prevent discolouration. Don't remove the chokes at this stage.

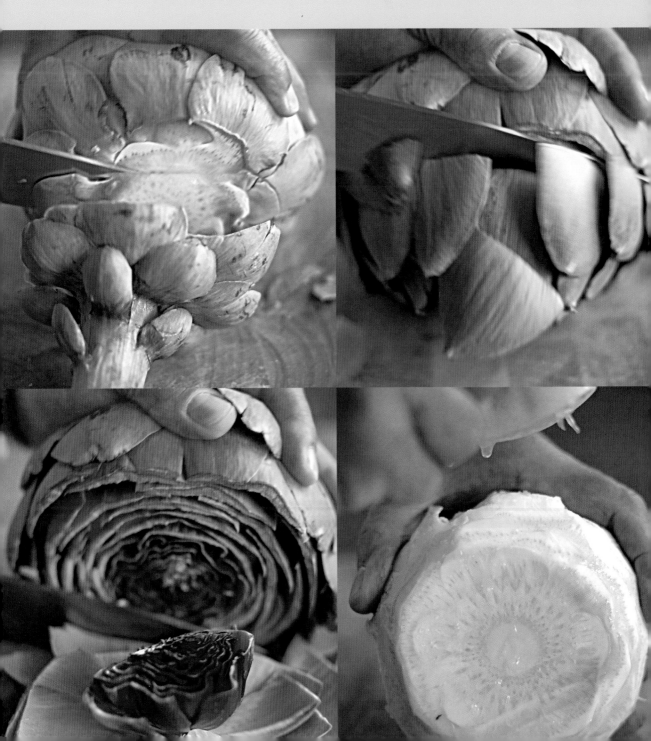

For the cooking liquor, mix 50g plain flour with 8 tbsp water to a paste in a large, wide pan. Gradually whisk in 1.5–2 litres water. Add 2–3 tsp salt, juice of 1 lemon, 1 chopped onion, 10 black peppercorns, 1 thyme sprig and a bay leaf. Bring to the boil, then add the artichokes, leafy side down, making sure they're fully submerged. Simmer for 15 minutes or until tender. Drain well.

When the artichokes are cool enough to handle, peel away the remaining tough leaves to expose the fibrous choke and remove this. Trim the edges to neaten – you will be left with a neatly shaped cup, which is the heart.

GLOBE ARTICHOKES A LA GRECQUE

Everyone has heard of mushrooms à la grecque. Try this dish – it's infinitely better!

4 globe artichokes
200g freshly podded
    broad beans

DRESSING
50ml white wine vinegar
125ml olive oil
125ml water
½ tsp coriander seeds,
    crushed
½ tsp white peppercorns,
    crushed
25g tomato purée
75ml lemon juice
10g garlic purée
few thyme sprigs
75g caster sugar
salt and pepper

TO SERVE
piece of Parmesan
25ml truffle oil

4 SERVINGS

1   First prepare the dressing. Put all the ingredients in a pan, season with a little salt and pepper and bring to a simmer. Allow to simmer gently for about 20 minutes, stirring occasionally, but do not boil.

2   Meanwhile, prepare and cook the artichokes (following the instructions on pages 18–19). Add them to the dressing and take off the heat. Set aside to marinate until cool. In the meantime, blanch the broad beans in boiling water for 3–4 minutes or until just tender. Drain, refresh under cold water and slip the beans out of their skins.

3   When the artichokes have cooled and you are almost ready to serve, add the broad beans. (Don't add them too early otherwise they will lose their beautiful green colour, owing to the vinegar.)

4   To serve, place an artichoke in the centre of each serving plate. Scatter the broad beans around and drizzle a little dressing over and around the artichokes. Shave some Parmesan over the artichokes and drizzle with the truffle oil. Serve immediately.

BRAISED ARTICHOKES WITH TOMATOES AND PANCETTA

Serve this as a starter, or as an accompaniment to grilled or barbecued lamb. It also works well with more robust fish dishes.

8 globe artichokes

4 plum tomatoes

2 tbsp olive oil

1 shallot, peeled and
chopped

70g pancetta, cubed

2 tsp chopped thyme
leaves

1–2 tbsp shredded basil
leaves

100ml dry white wine

100ml vegetable stock
(see page 248) or
chicken stock (see
page 247)

4 spring onions, trimmed
and shredded

salt and pepper

4 SERVINGS

1   Prepare and cook the artichokes (following instructions on pages 18–19). Cut them into quarters and set aside. Immerse the plum tomatoes in a bowl of boiling water for 15–30 seconds to loosen the skins, then drain and peel. Halve and deseed the tomatoes, then dice the flesh and reserve for later.

2   Heat a wide, shallow pan, add the olive oil and heat until it is almost smoking. Add the shallot and pancetta and fry over a medium heat for 5–6 minutes until the shallot has softened, stirring occasionally.

3   Add the artichokes and cook for 5 minutes, then add the thyme and half of the shredded basil, stirring well.

4   Pour in the wine and let bubble until reduced to a sticky consistency, then add the stock and reduce down by half. Tip the tomato dice into the pan and cook for a further 8–10 minutes or until the liquor thickens and the artichokes are well glazed.

5   Add the spring onions and season with salt and pepper to taste. Toss to mix and serve at once, sprinkled with the remaining shredded basil.

FENNEL

Aromatic, with a lovely sweet aniseed flavour, this is one of the strongest tasting of all vegetables and is very popular in Mediterranean countries. Homegrown fennel is available during the summer, but you can almost always buy this vegetable as it is grown in temperate climates year round.

When you are choosing fennel, look for fresh, white, unblemished tender bulbs with bright green feathery leaves. Dark green bulbs tend to have a bitter flavour and fennel with yellow patches is likely to be older, so best avoided. The plumper the bulb, the more succulent the flavour – long, thin bulbs are immature. Although bulbs often appear to be quite big, the outer layer is best removed as it can be stringy, so you need to allow for this when calculating quantities. Fennel is best eaten fresh, though it can be kept in the salad drawer of the fridge for up to 5 days.

To prepare fennel, cut off the root end, the feathery leaves and the outermost layer, as this is likely to be tough. Then simply cut the fennel into wedges or according to the recipe, or slice thinly if you are serving it raw. I like to braise fennel with aromatics, rather than simply boil it in water, for a greater depth of flavour.

Fennel can be served in so many different ways – to crisp up a salad, tossed in a vinaigrette, to partner cheese, or as an accompanying vegetable, especially to meaty fish, such as sea bass. And if you're in the mood for a smooth, flavoursome soup, try the one overleaf...

CREAM OF FENNEL SOUP

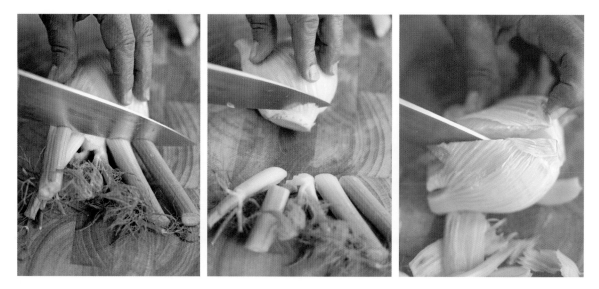

This velvety smooth, creamy soup has a superb flavour and is quick to prepare. I like to serve it before a fish main course, though it also makes a lovely light lunch with some good bread.

350g fennel bulbs

25g unsalted butter

3 large garlic cloves,
   peeled and sliced

110g potatoes, peeled and
   cut into chunks

2 leeks (white part only),
   washed and sliced

1/4 tsp fennel seeds

570ml chicken stock (see
   page 247)

salt and pepper

150ml single cream

150ml milk

4 SERVINGS

1   Trim and roughly chop the fennel bulbs, reserving the feathery tops for garnish. Melt the butter in a large pan, then add the fennel, garlic, potatoes, leeks and fennel seeds, stirring to coat in the butter. Cover and cook gently for 15 minutes.

2   Add the chicken stock and some salt and pepper and bring to a simmer. Cover the pan and simmer gently for 25 minutes.

3   Whiz the soup in a blender until smooth, then pass through a sieve into a clean pan and stir in the cream and milk. Reheat and adjust the seasoning.

4   Serve in warmed bowls, topped with the chopped reserved fennel tops.

BRAISED FENNEL

Braised in fish stock, fennel is an excellent accompaniment to bouillabaisse or grilled sea bass in a red wine sauce. To accompany chicken or red meat dishes, use chicken stock.

2 large fennel bulbs
50g unsalted butter
1 thyme sprig
1 bay leaf
1 strip orange zest
1 star anise
1 cardamom pod, lightly
  crushed
1 litre fish or chicken
  stock (see page 247)
salt and pepper

4–6 SERVINGS

1   Trim the base and tops off the fennel, peel the outer layer away and quarter each fennel bulb. Melt the butter in a large pan over a medium heat. Add the fennel and cook gently, without colouring for 4–5 minutes.

2   Add the thyme, bay leaf, orange zest and spices. Cook for another 5 minutes to release their aromatic flavours. Pour on the stock, bring to the boil and skim. Season with salt and pepper, cover and simmer over a low heat for about 10 minutes until the fennel is tender.

3   Remove the fennel with a slotted spoon to a warmed dish. Increase the heat under the pan and reduce the stock by half – no more or it might acquire a bitter taste.

4   Return the fennel to the stock and serve.

FENNEL AND CONFIT LEMON SALAD

This unusual salad is particularly delicious with grilled fish. I also like to serve it with crisp fried pieces of braised pork belly.

1 large fennel bulb
1 large lemon
salt and pepper
75g caster sugar
75ml tarragon vinaigrette
   (see page 250)

4 SERVINGS

1 Trim the base and top off the fennel and peel away the outer layer. Finely pare the zest from the lemon, avoiding the pith and set aside.

2 Using a mandolin, carefully slice the fennel lengthways, very thinly. Place the slices in a bowl of salted water with the juice from the lemon added and leave to stand for about 20 minutes to draw out excess water.

3 Cut the lemon zest into fine matchsticks, place in a small pan, cover with water and bring to the boil, then drain in a sieve. Repeat this process twice more (to take away the bitterness), then return to the cleaned pan. Add the sugar and 150ml water and bring to the boil, stirring to dissolve the sugar. Skim, then simmer until the liquor is syrupy. Allow to cool, then drain.

4 Drain the fennel shavings and mix with the confit lemon zest. Add the tarragon vinaigrette, toss well and serve.

TOMATOES

The most versatile ingredient in the kitchen, tomatoes have endless uses. They are great in salads, pasta dishes, soups, tarts, casseroles and chutneys... and much more. From the sweet concentrated flavour of the small cherry tomato right through to the big juicy beef tomatoes, there are so many different varieties. Sadly, most of the tomatoes on supermarket shelves are picked and shipped while still green, then artificially stimulated with ethylene gas, which reddens them but does nothing to stimulate the flavour. No wonder they are tasteless!

The best tomatoes are those bought during the summer months from farmers' markets or local greengrocers, or picked from the garden. You really will notice the difference in flavour so it's worth going the extra mile to source the tastiest around. If buying from a supermarket, vine-ripened organic tomatoes are your best option.

Fresh tomatoes should be bright red, firm and shiny without any cracks or wrinkles in the skin. If you're not planning on using the tomatoes for a couple of days, buy ones that are paler in colour and keep them in a cool place. A tip to hasten the ripening process is to place them in a paper bag and pop a red tomato into the batch.

Tomatoes can be baked, stuffed, roasted, fried, grilled, skewered, barbecued or slow-roasted and they will complement most dishes. One of my favourite ways to eat them is skinned, sliced, drizzled with olive oil, topped with thinly sliced onions and fresh shredded basil and devoured with warm ciabatta... delicious!

SUMMER ROASTED TOMATOES

These are brilliant with a summer barbecue. I like to add some black olives to the equation, but the simple recipe is delicious just as it is.

4 medium-large ripe, but
   firm tomatoes
   (preferably plum)
salt and pepper
2 tbsp olive oil

1 Halve the tomatoes horizontally and remove the core, seeds and juice. Season lightly. Heat the olive oil in a large non-stick pan (with a lid and suitable for use under the grill). Add the tomatoes, cut side down, and cook over a medium heat for about 5 minutes until the cut surface is lightly browned. Be careful not to burn them.

60g fresh white bread-
crumbs (slightly dry)

1–2 tsp crushed garlic

handful of parsley leaves,
finely chopped

4 tbsp extra virgin olive
oil

4 SERVINGS

2 Meanwhile, for the stuffing, combine the breadcrumbs, garlic, parsley and extra virgin olive oil in a bowl. Season generously with salt and pepper and mix well.

3 Turn the tomatoes cut side up and fill with the crumb mixture. Sprinkle with a little more salt and pepper. Partially cover the pan and cook until the tomatoes are tender, about 10 minutes. Meanwhile, preheat the grill.

4 Uncover the pan and place under the grill for a few minutes until the stuffing is golden and crunchy on top. Serve hot or at room temperature.

SPICY TOMATO SALAD

450g tomatoes (preferably
plum)

2 garlic cloves, peeled and
crushed

1 tbsp red wine vinegar

½ red onion, peeled and
chopped

1 red chilli, deseeded and
chopped

salt and pepper

3 tbsp extra virgin olive
oil

20 basil leaves, torn into
small pieces

4–6 SERVINGS

1 Immerse the tomatoes in a bowl of boiling water for 15–30 seconds to loosen the skins, then remove with a slotted spoon and peel. Halve the tomatoes, remove the seeds, then roughly chop the flesh.

2 Put the garlic, wine vinegar, red onion, chilli, a good pinch of salt and the olive oil into a small bowl and whisk to combine.

3 Tip the chopped tomatoes into a serving bowl and strain the dressing over them. Scatter over the basil leaves, season with salt and pepper to taste and toss to mix. Serve at once.

TOMATO STUFFED PEPPERS WITH ANCHOVIES AND MOZZARELLA

This is a great little supper dish, served simply with a salad and crusty bread. Alternatively, use it to accompany veal, lamb or beef dishes, and grilled or roasted turbot or sea bass.

4 red peppers
3 garlic cloves, peeled
16 ripe cherry tomatoes
salt and pepper
olive oil, to drizzle
6 anchovy fillets
1 ball of mozzarella,
    drained
15 large basil leaves, finely
    shredded

4 SERVINGS

1　Preheat the oven to 200°C/Gas 6. Halve the peppers lengthways, remove the seeds and cut out the white pith, then lay the peppers cut side up in a shallow ovenproof dish. Finely slice the garlic and put a few slices in each pepper half.

2　Cut the cherry tomatoes in half and stuff them into the pepper cavities. Season well with salt and pepper and drizzle with olive oil. Bake for about 45 minutes until soft and juicy.

3　Meanwhile, cut each anchovy fillet lengthways into 3 strips and the mozzarella roughly into 1cm cubes.

4　Place a few mozzarella cubes and a couple of anchovy strips on top of the cherry tomatoes. Return to the oven and bake for a further 5 minutes.

5　Scatter the shredded basil over the peppers and serve.

BEETROOT

This is a rich, sweet root vegetable that, in my view, is very underrated. Most people in this country are put off by those horrid jars of beetroot slices immersed in strong vinegar, which don't do justice to the fresh vegetable.

Beetroots come in all shapes and sizes. Apart from the familiar dark red globe beetroot, look out for golden and candy striped varieties, as well as long beetroot – shaped like carrots. All have a brilliant, smooth texture and are available all year (except early summer), though they taste sweeter during the winter months.

Select similar-sized beetroot, as these will cook more evenly. Generally, the younger and smaller they are, the sweeter and more delicate the flavour. Beetroot should be firm with undamaged skins. Leafy tops should be crisp, fresh and at least 5cm long, otherwise the colour is likely to leak into the cooking water. Beetroot is best eaten soon after buying, though it will keep for up to 2 weeks in the fridge.

To prepare, gently rinse beetroot to remove dirt, without damaging the skins. Either bake at 180°C/Gas 4 for about 1 hour, or simmer gently in water to cover until tender. This may take up to 1½ hours, depending on size. If you gently rub the skin and it comes away easily, the beetroot is cooked. Drain and peel when cool enough to handle.

I like to serve baked beetroot as a different accompaniment to meat dishes, especially roast duck. It also makes a vibrant, rich soup. Shredded raw beetroot is great mixed into a salad. And I love cooked baby beetroots, glazed and served with a fresh horseradish sauce.

GLAZED BEETROOT IN CIDER VINEGAR

This makes an attractive garnish to game and pork dishes. The syrup can be stored in the fridge in an airtight jar for up to 2 weeks.

2kg raw beetroot
160g caster sugar
225ml cider vinegar
salt

6–8 SERVINGS

1 First make the syrup. Peel and grate half of the raw beetroot and place in a saucepan. Add the sugar, pour on the cider vinegar and add 225ml water. Bring slowly to the boil, skim and simmer gently for about 20–25 minutes. By now, the beetroot will have released its colour and flavour.

2 Strain the mixture through a fine sieve into a clean pan, pushing with the back of a ladle to extract as much flavour as possible. Discard the residue in the sieve.

3 Bring the liquor to the boil and let bubble until reduced by a third to get a nice syrupy consistency, then pour into a bowl. (If not using straight away, cool, then store in a jar in the fridge.)

4 Cook the remaining beetroot in boiling salted water until tender. Drain in a colander and peel while still warm. Cut into 5mm dice and add to the beetroot syrup. Toss to coat well and set aside.

5 When ready to serve, tip the beetroot and syrup into a pan and place over a high heat for about 5 minutes, stirring occasionally, until the beetroot is beautifully glazed.

BEETROOT AND POTATO SALAD WITH SMOKED MACKEREL

This is a stunning salad. For a lunch or light supper, all it requires is a beautiful side salad, such as rocket and watercress tossed with a little tarragon vinaigrette (see page 250).

250g waxy potatoes, peeled

250g cooked beetroot

salt and pepper

2 shallots, peeled and finely diced

2 hard-boiled eggs, shelled and roughly diced

3 tbsp flat leaf parsley, chopped

2 large smoked mackerel fillets

DRESSING

3 tsp Dijon mustard

1$\frac{1}{2}$ tsp white wine vinegar

4 tbsp olive oil

HORSERADISH CREAM

75ml double cream

1 tsp white wine vinegar

2 tsp freshly grated horseradish

4 SERVINGS

1 Cut the potatoes and beetroot into 1cm dice, keeping them separate. Boil the diced potatoes in salted water for 7–10 minutes until just tender. Remove with a slotted spoon to a plate and set aside to cool. Repeat the process with the beetroot dice.

2 Put the potatoes into a large bowl and add the shallots, hard-boiled eggs and chopped parsley. (Don't add the beetroot yet, or the colours will run.)

3 To make the dressing, put the mustard and wine vinegar in a small bowl and whisk in the olive oil. Season with salt and pepper.

4 For the horseradish cream, whip the cream together with the wine vinegar and a little salt to soft peaks. Gently stir in the horseradish.

5 Just before serving, add the beetroot to the potato mixture and pour over the dressing. Peel the skin off the mackerel and flake the flesh into strips. Add to the salad and toss carefully to mix.

6 Pile the salad on to serving plates and top with a spoonful of horseradish cream. Drizzle any remaining dressing around the plates.

BABY BEETROOT WITH WARM GOAT'S CHEESE AND WALNUT DRESSING

12–16 baby beetroot,
   washed
4 Crottin de Chavignol
   (baby goat's cheeses),
   rind removed
salt and pepper
flour, for coating
2 eggs, beaten
200g fresh breadcrumbs
   (slightly dry)
50g caster sugar
50ml white wine vinegar
200ml walnut oil
sunflower oil, for deep-
   frying

GARNISH

1 head of chicory,
   separated into leaves
½ head of frisée, roughly
   torn
50ml walnut vinaigrette
   (see page 250)

4 SERVINGS

1   Put the beetroot in a saucepan, cover with water and bring to the boil. Lower the heat and cook gently until soft, 30–40 minutes depending on size. To check, pierce the beetroot with a sharp knife – they should be soft through to the middle. When ready, take off the heat and set aside to cool in the water. (This can be done a day ahead.)

2   Roll the goat's cheeses in seasoned flour to coat all over. One by one, dip into the beaten egg, then in the breadcrumbs to coat evenly.

3   Dissolve the sugar in the wine vinegar in a pan over a low heat, then bring to the boil and simmer to reduce by half. Allow to cool.

4   Drain the beetroot and peel off the skins, then place in a bowl. Mix the walnut oil with the reduced vinegar syrup and season. Pour over the beetroot and leave to marinate for at least 3 hours.

5   When ready to serve, preheat the oven to 200°C/Gas 6. Heat the sunflower oil in a suitable pan to 180°C. Deep-fry the goat's cheeses, two at a time, for about 5 minutes until golden. Remove with a slotted spoon and place on a baking tray. Finish cooking in the oven for 4–5 minutes.

6   Meanwhile, toss the salad leaves in the walnut dressing and arrange on plates. Place a hot goat's cheese in the centre and surround with the glazed beetroot. Drizzle some of the walnut marinade over the salad and serve at once.

POTATOES

These come in all sizes, textures and colours, but for a cook, the important distinction between varieties is whether they are floury or waxy. Floury potatoes, like Maris Piper and King Edward, mash and bake well, but don't hold their shape on boiling. In contrast, waxy potatoes, such as Charlotte and Cara, remain whole when boiled, but consequently don't mash well. Different varieties are better at different times of the year, so as long as the type of potato falls into the category you need, just buy whichever looks freshest and is therefore likely to be most flavoursome.

When you are buying new potatoes, choose those with ragged skins as this indicates they are fresh and will be easy to scrape. New potatoes lose flavour after a few days, so buy them in small quantities and cook them soon. In comparison, older potatoes can be stored in a cool, dark place for months. Here you should look for potatoes with some earth on and avoid any with green patches, which can be toxic. If there are green parts, cut them off. I would also avoid potatoes within plastic bags that show signs of condensation, as more often than not these have a slightly mouldy flavour.

Potatoes are versatile and can be boiled, mashed, steamed, roasted, baked or fried. Creamy mash complements all manner of dishes and is delicious flavoured with chopped herbs, grated horseradish or mustard. I don't think you can beat a bowl of freshly boiled baby new potatoes topped with melted butter, especially with new season's lamb. And dauphinoise potatoes are just divine, so give my recipe a go!

GLAZED POTATOES COOKED IN CIDER

8 even-sized small-
   medium potatoes
1 tbsp groundnut oil
salt and pepper
300ml dry cider
200ml chicken stock (see
   page 247)
1 garlic clove, peeled and
   crushed
1 thyme sprig
1 bay leaf
70g unsalted butter, diced

4 SERVINGS

1   Preheat the oven to 200°C/Gas 6. Peel the potatoes and immerse them in cold water as you do so.

2   Place a flameproof casserole over a medium heat. Drain the potatoes and pat dry on kitchen paper. Add the oil to the casserole, then the potatoes. Cook, turning occasionally, for about 5 minutes until lightly coloured.

3   Season the potatoes and pour over the cider and stock. Bring to the boil and add the garlic and herbs. Dot with the butter, turn the potatoes and place in the oven. Cook for about 40 minutes until tender, turning the potatoes every 10 minutes and checking after 30 minutes whether they're cooked. The liquor will reduce during cooking.

4   Transfer the potatoes to a warmed dish and keep warm. Place the casserole over a high heat and reduce the liquor down until syrupy. Add the potatoes and toss to glaze, then serve. An excellent accompaniment to roast pork.

ROSTI POTATOES

600g floury potatoes,
   such as Maris Piper or
   King Edward
salt and pepper
50ml clarified butter (see
   page 251)

4 SERVINGS

1   Preheat the oven to 200°C/Gas 6. Peel the potatoes and grate them, using a coarse grater. Season well with salt and pepper and squeeze out all the liquid.

2   Heat the butter in an ovenproof, non-stick frying pan. When hot, add the potatoes and spread out to a 20cm round (or shape into 4 individual cakes with a metal cutter). Fry over a medium heat until golden brown underneath, then flip over and fry for a further 2–3 minutes.

3   Transfer the pan to the oven, placing it on a low shelf and cook for about 15 minutes (or 10 minutes for individual ones) until crisp, golden and cooked through. Serve hot.

SPANISH BREAKFAST

This is a great brunch dish that works equally well for supper with some good rustic bread and a green salad on the side.

600g waxy new potatoes, such as Pink Fir or Charlotte

salt and pepper

200g cooking chorizo sausage

2 medium tomatoes

2 tbsp olive oil

1 small garlic clove, peeled and finely chopped

5 black olives, pitted and sliced

1 tbsp dry sherry

1 tsp sherry vinegar

splash of ordinary vinegar

4 eggs

1 tbsp flat leaf parsley, finely chopped

4 SERVINGS

1   Boil the potatoes in well salted water until just tender, about 15 minutes. Drain and cut into rounds, 1.5cm thick. Cut the chorizo sausage into rounds, the same thickness as the potatoes.

2   Briefly immerse the tomatoes in a bowl of boiling water to loosen the skins, then drain and peel. Halve, deseed and chop the tomatoes; set aside.

3   Heat a large frying pan over a medium-high heat and add the olive oil. Tip in the chorizo sausages and fry until lightly coloured and the oil begins to run. Add the potatoes to the pan and cook gently for a couple of minutes. Stir in the garlic and olives.

4   Mix together the sherry and sherry vinegar and pour into the pan. Take off the heat, but keep warm.

5   Bring a wide pan of water to the boil with a splash of vinegar added and swirl the water with a spoon to create a whirlpool. Crack an egg into a ramekin, then tip into the centre of the pan. Quickly add another egg in the same way. Turn the heat down to just simmering and poach for 3 minutes or until the yolks are just soft and the whites are slightly firm to the touch. Carefully remove with a slotted spoon to a warmed plate and keep warm, while you poach the other two eggs.

6   While the eggs are poaching, add the tomatoes and parsley to the potatoes, toss to mix and season well. Pile on to warmed plates and top each serving with a poached egg. Serve at once.

DAUPHINOISE POTATOES

This is probably my favourite potato accompaniment. It has the advantage that it can be prepared well ahead and left to cook slowly in the oven. It is particularly good with roasted lamb, such as my best end of lamb with caramelised orange and hazelnut salad (see page 164).

165ml milk

165ml double cream

handful of large garlic
   cloves, halved

700g floury potatoes,
   such as Maris Piper or
   King Edward

salt and pepper

30g butter

4–6 SERVINGS

1   Pour the milk and cream into a pan and add the garlic. Slowly bring to the boil, then take off the heat and set aside to infuse while you prepare the potatoes.

2   Preheat the oven to 150°C/Gas 2. Peel the potatoes and slice them very thinly on a mandolin.

3   Arrange a layer of potatoes in a round gratin dish or ovenproof sauté pan, measuring about 25cm. Season well with salt and pepper and strain over some of the infused creamy milk. Repeat the process with the rest of the potatoes. Drizzle any remaining liquor over the top.

4   Dot with the butter and cook in the oven for about 1½ hours until the potatoes are golden brown on the top and tender through when poked with the tip of a sharp knife. Serve piping hot.

LEEKS

These belong to the onion family, yet they have a far more subtle flavour and are generally sweeter than onions. Although available all year round, they are at their prime from October through to March. Leeks are extremely versatile and worthy of more than mere inclusion in soups and stocks, in my view.

When you buy leeks, examine them at both ends. The white part should be firm and unmarked and the green part should have erect foliage and a fresh colour. The smaller the leek, the more tender it will be. Because they have a strong aroma, leeks are best kept in a plastic bag in the fridge, so that they don't flavour other foods. They last well for about 5 days in the salad drawer.

Leeks need to be cleaned thoroughly before cooking as soil gets lodged between their layers. A good way to do this is to trim the hard ends from the green part and then split the leek lengthways, leaving about 3cm intact at the white base. Now fan out the leeks and wash well under cold running water. They can then be boiled, braised, steamed or sliced and stir-fried.

Leeks are a great accompanying vegetable, their distinctive flavour enhancing both meat and fish dishes. They can be eaten cold tossed in a vinaigrette, and they are excellent simply simmered in butter.

Leeks also lend themselves superbly to fillings for pies and tartlets, and warming winter soups. One of my favourite meals is succulent new season's lamb served with dauphinoise potatoes flavoured with chopped leeks and a little sage.

LEEK AND ASPARAGUS SALAD WITH TOASTED HAZELNUTS

This salad is so simple, yet so delicious! The ingredients complement each other perfectly.

24 pencil leeks, washed
salt and pepper
12 asparagus spears

DRESSING
300g crème fraîche
100ml hazelnut
   vinaigrette (see
   page 250)
30g hazelnuts, toasted
   and crushed

4 SERVINGS

1   Trim the pencil leeks, cutting off the roots if any, and any dark green leafy tops, then cut them in half. Bring a pan of salted water to the boil, plunge the leeks in and cook rapidly for 2–3 minutes until tender. Remove with a slotted spoon and spread out on a tray to cool quickly.

2   To make the dressing, pour the crème fraîche into a bowl and whisk lightly until smooth. Gradually stir in the vinaigrette, followed by the crushed hazelnuts and season with salt and pepper to taste.

3   When the leeks are cool, pat dry on a clean cloth or kitchen paper and place in a bowl. Pour over the crème fraîche dressing and mix gently.

4   Trim the base of the asparagus spears and peel the lower end of the stalks, then cut into 3cm lengths. Plunge into a pan of boiling salted water and cook for 2–3 minutes until just tender. Drain, refresh in iced water, then drain thoroughly.

5   Add the asparagus to the leek salad, toss to mix, then spoon on to plates. Serve as a starter.

LEEKS VINAIGRETTE WITH SUMMER TRUFFLE

The first new season's leeks are not much thicker than a pencil. They are wonderfully sweet, with a delicate flavour. Paired with the flavour of truffles, they are irresistible.

20 pencil leeks (or 8
    medium-small ones),
    trimmed and washed
salt and pepper

DRESSING
2 tbsp Dijon mustard
1 tbsp Pommery mustard
50ml white wine vinegar
pinch of sugar
300ml groundnut oil

TO FINISH
3 eggs, hard-boiled and
    peeled
25g chopped chives
20g white truffle, finely
    sliced, or a drizzle
    of truffle oil

4 SERVINGS

1 Bring a saucepan of salted water to the boil. If using medium-small leeks, cut them into 10cm lengths. Add the leeks to the pan and cook until very tender – approximately 3 minutes for pencil leeks, 8–10 minutes for medium-small ones. To test, pierce a leek with the point of a knife – it should easily pass all the way through. Drain thoroughly and set aside to cool.

2 To make the dressing, combine the mustards, wine vinegar, 5 tbsp water, the sugar and some seasoning in a bowl and whisk vigorously until smooth. Gradually whisk in the groundnut oil, drop by drop to begin with, then in a thin stream (as for mayonnaise) to make a smooth dressing – you can use a blender if you prefer. If the dressing is too thick, thin it down with a little more water.

3 Arrange the leeks in a shallow serving dish and pour over the dressing to cover them. Grate the hard-boiled eggs over the top and sprinkle with the chives. Finally, scatter over finely sliced truffle, or finish with a drizzle of truffle oil.

LEEK TARTLETS WITH POACHED QUAIL EGGS

These tartlets make an elegant starter or you can serve them as a light lunch with a salad and warm bread. I like to glaze them under the grill, but you can omit this stage if you like.

375g quantity shortcrust
   pastry (see page 251)

FILLING
4 medium leeks, trimmed
60g unsalted butter
bouquet garni (thyme,
   parsley, bay leaf)
200ml chicken stock (see
   page 247)
a little milk (if needed)
salt and pepper

1 To make the tartlet cases, roll out the shortcrust pastry thinly on a lightly floured surface and use to line four 10cm individual tartlet tins, pressing the pastry into the edges. Trim away excess pastry from the rims. Prick the bases with a fork, then rest in the fridge for 20 minutes. Meanwhile, preheat the oven to 190°C/Gas 5.

2 Line the pastry cases with greaseproof paper and baking beans, place on a baking sheet and bake blind for 15 minutes. Remove the paper and beans and return to the oven for 5–10 minutes or until the pastry bases are cooked. Transfer to a wire rack to cool.

TO ASSEMBLE

splash of white wine
  vinegar

16 quail's eggs

1 quantity hollandaise
  sauce (see page 249),
  warm

truffle oil, to drizzle
  (optional)

4 SERVINGS

3   To make the filling, thinly slice the leeks. Melt 50g butter in a pan over a medium heat, add the leeks with the bouquet garni and sweat for about 6–8 minutes to start to release their flavour. Add the chicken stock and simmer for about 20 minutes until the leeks are tender. Discard the bouquet garni.

4   Tip the leeks and liquor into a blender and whiz until smooth. Pass through a fine sieve into a warm bowl. If the purée is too thick, thin with a little milk. Finally stir in a knob of butter and check the seasoning. Keep warm.

5   Bring a wide, shallow pan of water to the boil and add a splash of vinegar. Once boiling, stir to create a whirlpool effect. Now poach the quail's eggs, four at a time. One by one, crack them into the pan and poach for 1½ minutes until the whites are set but the yolks are still soft. Carefully and immediately, lift them out with a slotted spoon and immerse in a bowl of ice-cold water to cool rapidly and keep soft. Repeat with the rest of the eggs.

6   To serve, preheat the grill. Fill the pastry cases with the warm leek purée. Reheat the soft poached quail's eggs by dipping them, one at a time, into boiling salted water for 10–20 seconds. Lift out, drain on kitchen paper and place 4 eggs in the centre of each tart case. Season with salt and pepper. Spoon the hollandaise sauce over the eggs, then briefly flash under the grill to glaze. Place on warmed plates and finish with a drizzle of truffle oil if you like.

COURGETTES

These are beautifully tender with a fresh delicate flavour, so it is hardly surprising that they have become so popular. Summer, when homegrown courgettes are around, is definitely the best time to cook them, though they are flown in from warmer climes throughout the year.

Look for courgettes with firm, shiny skins, without any blemishes. Smaller courgettes are sweeter and more succulent than larger ones. The bigger they get, the more stringy and bland the flesh becomes. Also, look out for the yellow variety as these courgettes have a sweeter taste and add colour to a meal. For a short while in the summer, courgette flowers are available, though, regrettably, not to the same extent that you find in Italy. These yellow trumpets with their tiny, baby courgettes attached are delicious stuffed and baked, steamed or deep-fried.

Courgettes are best eaten within a few days of buying, so refrigerate and eat them soon. To prepare, trim off the ends, cut into the required lengths or into batons and you're ready to go.

This vegetable can be cooked in so many ways – blanched, stuffed, baked, fried, even roasted. It is also very successful cooked in the microwave, just with a knob of butter. Pan-fry courgette slices in a little butter or olive oil with some garlic for a summer accompaniment. Or dip courgette sticks into flour or batter, deep-fry and then plunge into your favourite dips for a tasty appetiser or snack. I also love a light, fresh courgette soup with wholemeal bread and butter.

TEMPURA OF BABY COURGETTES

16 baby courgettes,
    preferably with flowers
    attached
salt and cayenne pepper
sunflower oil, for deep-
    frying

BATTER
90g plain flour
60g cornflour
30g baking powder
250ml sparkling water,
    chilled
8 ice cubes

4 SERVINGS

1   Top and tail the courgettes. With a sharp knife, make a series of incisions, about 2mm apart, along two-thirds of the length of the courgettes, keeping them intact at one end. Season with a little salt and cayenne pepper and leave to stand for about 10 minutes.

2   For the batter, mix the dry ingredients together in a bowl, then slowly add the water, mixing with a fork or chopsticks. Don't worry if there are a few small lumps; this is normal. Finally add the ice cubes to keep it cool.

3   Heat the oil in a wok or deep pan to 170–180°C. Draw the courgettes, one at a time, through the batter, immerse in the hot oil and deep-fry for 30 seconds–1 minute until golden brown. Remove and drain on kitchen paper. Repeat with the rest.

4   Serve straight away with a light tarragon mayonnaise (see page 250), spicy tomato dip or soy sauce.

COURGETTES WITH DILL AND MINT

900g courgettes, trimmed
60ml extra virgin olive oil
1 onion, peeled and diced
salt and pepper
1 tbsp crushed garlic
120ml chicken stock (see
    page 247)
4 tbsp each dill and mint
    leaves, chopped

6 SERVINGS

1   Cut the courgettes into 2cm cubes. Heat the olive oil in a large pan over a medium-high heat. Add the onion and cook for a few minutes to soften slightly. Add the courgettes, season and cook, stirring occasionally, until they have softened slightly and begun to brown. Stir in the garlic and cook for a couple of minutes.

2   Add the stock, lower the heat, cover and simmer for 5 minutes or until the courgettes are tender. Stir in the herbs and check the seasoning.

3   Serve either hot or cold as an accompaniment, or toss through pasta.

COURGETTE FLOWERS STUFFED WITH DARTMOUTH CRAB

This is a popular dish at The New Angel during the short courgette flower season. It certainly has visual appeal and I love the combination of flavours. Courgette flowers are very delicate and should be eaten on the day you buy them.

12 baby courgettes with
    flowers attached
120g baby spinach leaves,
    washed
salt and pepper

STUFFING

10 medium scallops
1 egg
100ml double cream
pinch of cayenne pepper
500g fresh white crab
    meat
1 tbsp shredded basil

TO SERVE

25g unsalted butter
200ml fish vinaigrette
    (see page 250)
1–2 tomatoes, skinned,
    deseeded and diced
chervil or parsley sprigs,
    to garnish

4–6 SERVINGS

1   Carefully open out the courgette flowers and cut out the stamen from the centre of each. Slice the courgettes from top to bottom at 2mm intervals, leaving 1cm intact at the flower end, to make a fan. Set aside.

2   Cook the spinach with just the water clinging to the leaves after washing until it is just starting to wilt, then drain and set aside.

3   To make the stuffing, blitz the scallops in a blender or food processor to a smooth paste. Add the egg and cream and whiz to a velvety purée. Transfer to a bowl and season with a little salt and cayenne pepper. Mix in the crab meat and basil.

4   Carefully spoon the filling into the courgette flowers and very carefully twist the ends with your fingertips to seal. Place the courgettes in a steamer over a pan of boiling water, cover and steam for about 5–6 minutes until the stuffed flowers feel firm to the touch. (You may need to cook them in batches.)

5   Meanwhile, melt the butter in a pan, add the spinach and reheat gently, seasoning with salt and pepper to taste.

6   Warm the vinaigrette in another pan, but do not boil. Add the tomato dice and check the seasoning.

7   To serve, spoon the spinach into the centre of each warmed plate. Place 2 or 3 courgettes on top and spoon the tomato and vinaigrette over and around. Garnish with sprigs of chervil.

PUMPKIN AND SQUASH

Available in all different shapes, sizes and colours, these are more or less interchangeable in recipes, which means you can use the tastiest variety available to you at any given time. Brilliant! Mention pumpkin and, like most of you I'm sure, I think of Halloween with my kids – taking home the biggest pumpkin I can find, removing the flesh, then cutting out holes to make a face even uglier than mine!

In fact, pumpkin really is an excellent vegetable for the winter months. It keeps remarkably well and the attractive orange flesh is very sweet tasting. As with all varieties of squash, go for smaller pumpkins as these will have a higher proportion of flesh to seeds than their larger counterparts. The skin should be smooth and firm. This vegetable can be stored in a cool dark place for up to a month.

Pumpkin and other winter squashes are usually peeled before cooking. They can be baked, boiled, mashed or roasted. The seeds are often added to breads and the flesh is good for thickening up stews and pies. I like to slice mine in half, bake them in the oven and then scoop out the flesh from the skins. Then I simply toss it with some butter and serve with lemon marinated grilled chicken.

If you boil squash, do so in a tiny amount of water, for a more intense flavour. Mash and use as an alternative to potatoes, but don't blanch squash before roasting as it will just fall apart in the tray. Probably my favourite way to cook squash is to cut it into wedges, throw around a juicy joint of beef and roast in the meat juices… delicious.

PUMPKIN SOUP

I like to serve this comforting soup topped with garlic croûtons, which I make by pan-frying thin slices of baguette in olive oil and butter flavoured with a little crushed garlic.

2kg pumpkin

100ml olive oil

2 large onions, peeled and
  chopped

2 large carrots, peeled and
  chopped

2 garlic cloves, peeled and
  chopped

1 thyme sprig

1 bay leaf

1 litre chicken stock (see
  page 247)

60g unsalted butter

2 tsp kirsch

salt and pepper

¼ tsp freshly grated
  nutmeg

TO SERVE

garlic croûtons (optional,
  see above)

chopped parsley

4–6 SERVINGS

1 Peel, deseed and dice the pumpkin. Heat the olive oil in a large pan until just smoking. Add the pumpkin, onions and carrots and cook over a medium heat for 6–8 minutes or until they start to colour. Add the garlic, thyme and bay leaf and cook for a further 5 minutes.

2 Add the stock and bring to the boil. Skim, then lower the heat and simmer for 30 minutes or until the pumpkin is soft. Discard the herbs.

3 Purée the soup in a blender until smooth, in batches as necessary, adding the butter as you do so, to give a velvety texture. Pass the soup through a fine sieve into a clean pan and reheat gently. Add the kirsch and season with salt, pepper and nutmeg to taste.

4 Pour the soup into warmed bowls and scatter with garlic croûtons if you like. Sprinkle with chopped parsley and serve.

PUMPKIN RISOTTO WITH SAGE AND PARMESAN

This is my favourite winter risotto. The flavours of roasted pumpkin, sage and Parmesan come together brilliantly and the creamy texture is divine.

800g pumpkin

50ml olive oil

8 sage leaves

salt and pepper

1 litre chicken stock (see page 247)

100g unsalted butter

3 shallots, peeled and finely diced

1 large garlic clove, peeled and finely diced

350g risotto rice, such as arborio

50ml dry white wine

100g Parmesan, freshly grated

4 SERVINGS

1   Preheat the oven to 200°C/Gas 6. Peel and deseed the pumpkin, then cut into 5cm cubes. Place in a roasting tray with the olive oil and sage leaves and toss to coat in the oil. Season well with salt and pepper, cover the tray with foil and roast in the oven for 45 minutes.

2   Bring the stock to the boil in a pan, lower the heat and keep it at a low simmer.

3   Melt half of the butter in a heavy-based pan. Add the shallots and garlic and cook gently for about 6–8 minutes until soft and translucent. Add the rice and stir well to coat all the grains in the butter. Pour in the wine and stir until it is all absorbed.

4   Pour a ladleful of the hot stock into the pan and stir until absorbed. Repeat this process until all the rice grains are tender, yet still individual and retaining a slight bite. This will take about 15–20 minutes; you may not need all of the stock.

5   Add the roasted pumpkin to the risotto, along with the remaining butter and Parmesan. Stir carefully to mix.

6   Serve the risotto on warmed plates, with a crisp salad on the side.

PUMPKIN AND BEETROOT SALAD

This mouthwatering salad makes a delicious lunch or light supper, served with some good, rustic bread. Picos is an excellent blue cheese from the Picos de Europa mountain range in northern Spain. It has a mature flavour and a creamy, soft texture, but if you cannot find it, simply use dolcelatte or Roquefort instead.

900g pumpkin or
   1 butternut squash
olive oil, for cooking and
   drizzling
salt and pepper
1 medium beetroot,
   peeled
few thyme sprigs
1 tbsp sherry vinegar
25g unsmoked bacon,
   derinded and cut into
   thin strips
1 head of radicchio,
   shredded
squeeze of lemon juice
25g Picos blue cheese

4 SERVINGS

1   Preheat the oven to 200°C/Gas 6. Peel and deseed the pumpkin, then cut into thick slices. Place on a roasting tray, drizzle with a little olive oil, season and toss well. Roast in the oven for about 40 minutes until golden and tender, turning halfway through cooking.

2   Meanwhile, cut the beetroot into 8 wedges. Place on a piece of foil with the thyme. Drizzle with olive oil and the sherry vinegar and season well. Wrap in the foil and bake alongside the pumpkin for about 30 minutes until tender.

3   Blanch the bacon in a pan of boiling water for 3 minutes to draw out excess salt and impurities. Drain and pat dry. Fry the bacon pieces in a little olive oil until golden and starting to crisp. Remove and drain on kitchen paper.

4   Cut the beetroot and pumpkin into chunks and place in a large bowl with the radicchio, bacon and any juice from the beetroot. Drizzle with a little olive oil, add a squeeze of lemon juice and season well. Toss to mix, then divide among plates and crumble over the blue cheese to serve.

MUSHROOMS

These are really the fruiting bodies of fungi, which may not sound too appetising, but I love them and they are an integral part of many of my recipes. There are hundreds of edible varieties, but from a cook's perspective they are either cultivated, like button and chestnut mushrooms, or wild, such as cep, chanterelle and morel. For the recipes in this book you can use any kind – just select the freshest and best you can find.

Mushrooms deteriorate quickly, so buy only as many as you'll use within a few days, or less in the case of wild varieties. Avoid cultivated ones (except chestnuts) that have turned brown. Until ready to cook, keep on a tray in the fridge, covered with kitchen paper.

As mushrooms don't keep well, various preserving methods have emerged, notably drying. Dried ceps, porcini, chanterelles and morels are widely available and lend an intense flavour to dishes.

Cultivated mushrooms are usually very clean: usually you just need to wipe them with damp kitchen paper. Wild mushrooms need more thorough cleaning: trim off stems, brush off grit with a soft brush, rinse quickly under cold running water and pat dry. Dried mushrooms need to be pre-soaked in warm water for about 20 minutes.

Button mushrooms are good thrown into casseroles, soups and sauces. I like to add chopped chestnut mushrooms raw to salads, or use them to make a topping for crostini. When wild mushrooms are in season, I love to pan-fry them in butter with shallots and garlic. And dried mushrooms are great in pasta and rice dishes, soups and stuffings.

DUXELLE OF FIELD MUSHROOMS

This mixture is great for filling tomatoes or tartlet cases. I also like to use it to stuff ravioli and tortellini.

250g wild mushrooms or
   field mushrooms
40g unsalted butter
4 shallots, peeled and
   finely diced
1 garlic clove, peeled and
   finely diced
5 tarragon leaves, finely
   chopped
2 tbsp white wine
100ml double cream
salt and pepper
squeeze of lemon juice, to
   taste

ABOUT 4 SERVINGS

1   Wash the mushrooms carefully under cold running water to remove any grit and pat dry with kitchen paper. Cut the mushrooms and their stalks into 5mm dice.

2   Melt the butter in a pan and fry the shallots and garlic over a gentle heat until soft and translucent. Add the mushrooms and tarragon and turn up the heat. Cook for 5 minutes or so, until all the moisture has evaporated.

3   Add the wine and let bubble until the liquor has completely evaporated. Add the cream and cook until reduced and thickened slightly. Season well with salt and pepper. Add a few drops of lemon juice to lift the flavour and cut the richness.

4   Use to fill tartlets, stuff tomatoes or peppers prior to baking or to fill pasta.

MUSHROOM BRUSCHETTA

These bruschetta are incredibly tasty and easy to prepare – perfect for lunch or a substantial snack. I use the same topping on toasted thin baguette slices, to serve as an appetiser with drinks. And the mixture is equally good tossed through hot pasta. Any fresh, tasty mushrooms can be used and to vary the flavour you can use chopped basil or parsley instead of rosemary.

450g ripe tomatoes

450g chestnut (or other) mushrooms, cleaned

2 garlic cloves, peeled and crushed

1 tsp tender rosemary leaves, finely chopped

3 tbsp lemon juice

120ml extra virgin olive oil

salt and pepper

TO SERVE

1 ciabatta loaf

4–8 SERVINGS

1   Cut out the core from the tomatoes. Halve, deseed and chop the flesh and place in a bowl.

2   Cut the mushrooms into small dice and add to the tomatoes with the garlic, rosemary, lemon juice and olive oil. Cover and leave to stand for at least 30 minutes or up to an hour at room temperature.

3   Preheat the grill. Season the mushroom mixture with salt and pepper to taste. Halve the ciabatta lengthways and cut each half into 2 or 4 pieces (depending on appetite). Toast until lightly golden on both sides.

4   Pile the mushroom mixture on top of the ciabatta and return to the grill until bubbling and golden. Alternatively, warm the bruschetta through in a preheated oven at 180°C/Gas 4 for 5–10 minutes before serving.

POTATO PANCAKES WITH MUSHROOM TOPPING

This is a great way to serve fresh ceps when they are in season, otherwise fresh chestnut mushrooms work well.

POTATO PANCAKES

250g floury potatoes, such as King Edward

salt and pepper

25ml milk

1 tbsp plain flour

1 tbsp double cream

1 large egg

2 large egg whites

groundnut oil, for frying

MUSHROOM TOPPING

300ml chicken stock

100ml walnut oil

1 garlic clove, peeled and crushed

squeeze of lemon juice, to taste

200g fresh mushrooms, such as ceps or chestnut mushrooms, cleaned

1 tbsp flat leaf parsley, finely chopped

4 SERVINGS

1 For the pancakes, boil the potatoes in their skins in salted water until tender. Drain and leave until cool enough to handle. Peel off the skins and put the potatoes through a ricer into a large bowl, or use a potato masher to mash them smoothly, making sure you get rid of any lumps. Mix in the milk, flour, cream and the whole egg, and season well with salt and pepper.

2 To make the dressing for the mushrooms, pour the stock into a pan and boil rapidly to reduce to 100ml. Add the walnut oil, garlic and lemon juice. Bring back to the boil, remove from the heat and set aside to cool for about 10 minutes. Season with salt and pepper to taste.

3 Carefully slice the mushrooms finely, into 2mm thick slices. Place them in a bowl with the chopped parsley and pour over the dressing. Leave to marinate while you finish the pancakes.

4 Whisk the egg whites in a clean bowl to soft peaks. Stir half of this into the potato mixture, then carefully fold in the rest. Adjust the seasoning if necessary.

5 Heat a little groundnut oil in a large non-stick frying pan over a medium heat. Ladle in the potato mixture, to make 4 rounds (cook in batches if your pan isn't big enough). Cook for 2–3 minutes until the pancakes are golden brown underneath, then turn with a spatula and cook for a further 2–3 minutes. If cooking in batches, keep the pancakes warm in a low oven while you cook the rest.

6 Meanwhile, lightly warm the mushrooms in their dressing. Place a pancake on each warmed serving plate. Using a slotted spoon, pile the mushrooms on top. Surround with a generous drizzle of dressing and serve at once.

PEAS

These herald the arrival of summer when they start to appear in our local markets. The flavour of young, fresh peas matches their vibrant colour and I adore them.

Peas are native to the Mediterranean and grow on climbing plants in all different sizes and textures. Traditional English or European peas are round with thin skins and are invariably shelled before cooking. In contrast, sugar snaps and mangetout are eaten whole. Sugar snap peas have more of a crunch, while mangetout (or snow peas) are flat and wide with smaller seeds.

Whichever type of pea you buy, look for firm, bright green pods and avoid any that are wrinkled or discoloured. Fresh peas lose half their sugar within a few hours at room temperature, so I recommend that you shell and cook them as soon as possible. If you need to keep them for longer than 12 hours, pod the peas and keep them chilled. To shell peas, simply press the pods open with your fingers, then use your thumb to push out the peas.

Fresh peas are easily spoiled by overcooking, so cook until just tender. Even larger peas only take about 10 minutes in boiling water. You can always plunge them into cold water once cooked and reserve until later – this helps to keep their flavour, colour and texture.

Peas tossed with butter and fresh mint are a great accompaniment to lamb. I like to add sugar snaps to stir-fries to add bite, and blanched mangetout are great in a salad. Pea and ham soup is a really tasty treat during the summer months too.

PEAS WITH PANCETTA

I always try to make the most of fresh peas during their short season. This accompaniment is particularly good with chicken, game and meaty white fish dishes.

1kg fresh peas in their
    pods, shelled
salt and pepper
100g smoked pancetta,
    cut into strips
15g butter
handful of mint leaves,
    roughly torn

4 SERVINGS

1 Add the peas to a large pan of boiling salted water and boil for 5–8 minutes or until just tender. Drain well.

2 Blanch the pancetta pieces in a pan of boiling water for 2 minutes to remove excess salt and impurities. Drain and pat dry on kitchen paper.

3 Melt the butter in a sauté pan over a very low heat, add the pancetta and cook until golden brown. Add the peas and torn mint leaves and cook for 5 minutes, stirring every now and then.

4 Now season with pepper to taste. Transfer to a warmed dish and serve at once.

MANGETOUT WITH GINGER

A final drizzle of hot sesame oil lends a special flavour to these simple stir-fried peas. Serve as an accompaniment to oriental-style chicken or fish dishes.

1 tbsp groundnut oil
1 tsp grated fresh root
    ginger
225g mangetout,
    trimmed
1 tbsp soy sauce
1 tbsp dark sesame oil
salt and pepper

4 SERVINGS

1 Place a wok or non-stick sauté pan over a high heat and add the groundnut oil. When it is hot, add the ginger and mangetout and cook, stirring occasionally, for about 2 minutes until lightly browned. Add the soy sauce, toss well and transfer to a warmed bowl.

2 Add the sesame oil to the pan and heat briefly, for about 10 seconds. Pour over the mangetout, season with salt and pepper and serve immediately.

TAGLIATELLE WITH PEAS, BROAD BEANS AND ARTICHOKES

I love this pasta dish with its fresh spring flavours. You can, of course, vary the vegetables, replacing the artichokes with blanched asparagus spears if you like, and perhaps adding some baby carrots for colour.

500g fresh broad beans in
    their pods, shelled
salt and pepper
4 tbsp olive oil
1 onion, peeled and
    chopped
1/2 Little Gem lettuce,
    shredded
125ml vegetable stock
400g egg tagliatelle
500g fresh peas in their
    pods, shelled
2 mint sprigs, torn
4 prepared and cooked
    artichoke hearts (see
    pages 18–19), quartered
4 tbsp pine nuts, toasted
100g Parmesan, freshly
    grated

4 SERVINGS

1　Blanch the broad beans in a large pan of boiling salted water for about 3 minutes until just tender. Remove and plunge into a bowl of iced water to cool quickly. Drain and slip them out of their tough outer skins to reveal the emerald green tender beans inside.

2　Heat 2 tbsp olive oil in a pan, add the onion and cook gently until soft. Add the shredded lettuce and sauté briefly until wilted. Pour in the stock and bring to the boil.

3　In the meantime, cook the tagliatelle in a large pan of boiling salted water until al dente.

4　Tip the peas on to the lettuce and onion, stir and simmer for a few minutes until tender. Add the broad beans and mint and season with salt and pepper to taste. Add the artichokes and heat through.

5　Drain the pasta and toss with the remaining 2 tbsp olive oil. Pile the vegetables into warmed shallow bowls and scatter over the toasted pine nuts. Swirl the pasta into nests and place on top. Sprinkle with some of the Parmesan and grind over a little pepper.

6　Serve at once, handing the rest of the Parmesan around for guests to help themselves.

PULSES

I use pulses extensively because I love the way they absorb flavours during cooking, especially richly flavoured stocks. I use many different varieties, including white haricot beans, flecked borlotti beans, pale green flageolets and lentils. My chefs favour the French green Puy lentils, but I prefer the slightly smaller brown Castelluccio lentils from Umbria in Italy.

Pulses can be a nutritious meal in their own right, but they also make a great accompaniment to meat and fish dishes. Try serving them as a tasty alternative to rice or potatoes.

Dried pulses have the advantage that they keep well for a long time, although older pulses will take longer to cook than freshly bought ones. Also, most dried beans and peas need to be soaked in cold water for around 12 hours before cooking, so you'll need to think ahead. Once soaked, pulses will at least double in weight. This means you need to allow about 50g dried weight per person.

Pulses play a role in so many dishes. I like to simmer haricot beans with a bacon bone and garlic to use for a minestrone. I also cook pulses in a good chicken stock with herbs, then add cream to serve as a winter soup, topped with garlic croûtons. Braised lentils flavoured with a little crispy bacon, chopped shallots, diced tomato and parsley will complement any fish or meat dish. And a purée of flageolet beans is wonderful with braised lamb. Chilli con carne may have been around forever, but it is a great dish, if prepared well. However, there is really nothing to surpass a proper cassoulet from southwest France.

CANNELLINI BEANS WITH PEPPERS AND COURGETTE

This accompaniment goes well with most fish and meat dishes. I often serve steamed sea bass fillets on top of the beans, surrounding them with a basil butter sauce. The effect is stunning (see page 125).

200g dried cannellini or
    haricot beans

1.5 litres chicken stock

1 shallot, peeled and
    halved

1 carrot, peeled and
    halved

1 small leek, halved and
    washed

1 celery stick, halved

1 garlic clove, peeled and
    crushed

1 thyme sprig

1 bay leaf

$1/2$ red pepper

$1/2$ yellow pepper

150g fennel, trimmed

1 courgette, trimmed

salt and pepper

large knob of unsalted
    butter

few basil leaves, shredded

4 SERVINGS

1 Put the beans in a bowl, pour on cold water to cover and leave to soak overnight.

2 The next day, drain the soaked beans and put them in a saucepan with the stock, shallot, carrot, leek, celery, garlic, thyme and bay leaf. Bring to the boil, skim off any scum from the surface and then simmer for $1-1^{1}/2$ hours or until the beans are soft to the touch and tender through.

3 Pick out and discard the herbs and vegetables, reserving the beans in the stock until later.

4 Using a swivel vegetable peeler, peel away the skin from the peppers, discard the white pith and seeds and cut the flesh into 1cm dice. Remove the outer layer from the fennel and quarter the courgette lengthways, then cut both vegetables into 1cm pieces.

5 Blanch the peppers, courgette and fennel separately in a pan of lightly salted boiling water for 1 minute. Remove with a slotted spoon and refresh in iced water, then drain on kitchen paper.

6 To serve, mix the peppers, fennel and courgette dice through the beans. Warm through gently, then add the butter and shredded basil. Check the seasoning and serve.

ITALIAN LENTILS WITH SMOKED BACON, SHALLOTS AND PARSLEY

I love lentils. Everyone says Puy lentils from France are the best, but I find the little pale brown Castelluccio lentils from Italy have a sweeter taste. Cooked, as here, with smoked bacon and flavouring vegetables, they taste divine. Try them with pan-fried scallops or braised pork, or serve as an alternative vegetable accompaniment to chicken or lamb.

100g Castelluccio lentils

1 tbsp olive oil

½ onion, peeled and
   halved

1 carrot, peeled and
   halved

1 celery stick, halved

½ leek, trimmed, split
   and washed

1 garlic clove, peeled and
   sliced

2 thyme sprigs

1 bay leaf

50g piece smoked bacon

500ml chicken stock (see
   page 247)

50g bacon lardons

30g unsalted butter, diced

2 shallots, peeled and
   finely chopped

30g flat leaf parsley,
   chopped

salt and pepper

25ml tarragon vinaigrette
   (see page 250), optional

4 SERVINGS

1   Wash the lentils in a sieve under cold running water, drain and set aside.

2   Heat the olive oil in a large pan and sweat the onion, carrot, celery and leek with the garlic, thyme and bay leaf for a few minutes.

3   Add the lentils and piece of smoked bacon, then pour on the stock to cover. Bring to the boil, skim off any scum from the surface and lower the heat. Simmer for about 30–40 minutes until the lentils are tender. Drain the lentils, discarding the flavouring vegetables and bacon, but reserving the stock for later.

4   Place a non-stick frying pan over a medium-high heat. Add the bacon lardons with the butter and cook until they are golden and crisp.

5   Add the lentils and a quarter of the reserved liquor. Let bubble until the liquor has reduced by half, then add the shallots and parsley. Check the seasoning and stir in the tarragon dressing, if using, to serve.

FLAGEOLET BEAN AND SHELLFISH SALAD

100g dried flageolet beans

500ml chicken stock (see
   page 247)

1 shallot, peeled and sliced

1 bay leaf

1 thyme sprig

1 garlic clove, halved
   (unpeeled)

SHELLFISH

50 fresh mussels, cleaned

40 fresh clams, cleaned

1 onion, peeled

1 leek, trimmed and
   washed

1 carrot, peeled

1 celery stick

5 tbsp olive oil

1 garlic clove, peeled and
   finely chopped

1 thyme sprig

2 flat leaf parsley sprigs

1 tsp black peppercorns

100g cleaned squid

1 red chilli, deseeded and
   finely chopped

juice of $\frac{1}{2}$ lemon

salt and pepper

TO FINISH

3 tbsp chopped flat leaf
   parsley

4 SERVINGS

1 Put the beans in a bowl, pour on cold water to cover and leave to soak overnight.

2 The next day, drain the beans and put them in a pan with the stock, shallot, bay leaf, thyme and garlic. Bring to the boil, skim off any scum and simmer for 35–45 minutes or until tender.

3 To prepare the shellfish, check that the cleaned mussels and clams are closed. Tap any that are open firmly and discard if they don't shut.

4 Chop the vegetables. Heat 2 tbsp olive oil in a large pan, which has a tight-fitting lid, then add the vegetables, garlic, herbs and peppercorns. Add 5–6 tbsp water and bring to the boil. Tip in the mussels and clams, cover with the lid and steam until the shellfish open. This should take 4–5 minutes. Drain in a large colander set over a bowl to save the juices.

5 Remove the mussels and clams from their shells and discard any that remain closed. Strain the cooking juices through a muslin-lined sieve into a small pan. Open out the squid pouches and score the flesh, then cut into strips. Bring the juices to the boil, then add the squid strips and tentacles. Turn off the heat, cover and leave for 2$\frac{1}{2}$ minutes – the squid will cook in the residual heat. Remove with a slotted spoon and set aside.

6 Drain the beans, discarding the herbs and garlic, then place in a large bowl with the mussels, clams, squid and red chilli. To make the dressing, mix 25ml of the cooking liquor with the remaining 50ml olive oil and the lemon juice. Taste and adjust the seasoning (salt might not be needed, but pepper is a must). Pour the dressing over the shellfish and leave to stand for 5 minutes.

7 To serve, divide the salad among shallow bowls and sprinkle with the chopped parsley. Serve warm or at room temperature if you prefer.

FISH & SHELLFISH

MUSSELS, CLAMS, COCKLES & SCALLOPS

I can go to Wonwell, my favourite beach in the whole of Devon, and gather some of the most beautiful little mussels, cockles, clams and even razor clams at low tide. However, in my experience, the best mussels are rope-grown in tidal waters. These 'farmed' mussels are always free of grit and sand, and they taste much sweeter.

The main rule when buying shellfish is to buy from a seafood specialist with a high turnover. Fresh molluscs should be alive when you buy them. Their shells shouldn't be damaged, and they should either be closed, or if you tap them firmly, they should shut tightly. Once you have got them home, immerse the molluscs in cold water, as this will help rid them of any sand and grit before you cook them.

The second rule is to cook molluscs soon after purchase – on the day you buy them, or at least within 24 hours. With mussels, the colour is an indication of sex rather than quality. Bright orange mussels are female, beige ones are generally male.

Most importantly, don't overcook molluscs. Steam mussels, clams and cockles just long enough to open them. Shelled scallops are equally sensitive – steam, pan-fry or grill them, but only briefly otherwise you'll ruin their delicate texture. An overcooked mollusc is more like a rubber ball, which the human body isn't designed to digest!

A glass of cold, crisp white wine is the ideal complement to shellfish, so make sure you have a bottle chilling in the fridge.

MUSSELS IN COCONUT MILK WITH CORIANDER AND CHILLIES

This is definitely one of my favourite dishes. I always enjoy a bowl of steaming mussels and cooking them with oriental flavourings takes them to a whole new level. Try it!

3kg fresh mussels, cleaned

1 tsp black peppercorns

2 tsp coriander seeds

1 tsp cumin seeds

½ tsp ground turmeric

3 tsp ground almonds

1 tbsp sunflower oil

1 small onion, peeled and thinly sliced

1cm piece fresh root ginger, peeled and finely chopped

2 garlic cloves, peeled and finely chopped

4 green (or red) chillies, deseeded and sliced

200ml coconut milk

200ml fish stock (see page 247)

1 tbsp tamarind water (see right)

handful of coriander, roughly chopped

salt and pepper

juice of 1 lime, or to taste

4 SERVINGS

1 Set the cleaned mussels aside, discarding any that are open and don't close when sharply tapped. Using a spice grinder or pestle and mortar, grind together the peppercorns, coriander and cumin seeds, turmeric and ground almonds.

2 Heat the sunflower oil in a large pan. Add the onion, ginger and garlic and fry gently for 5 minutes. Add the ground spice mix and fry for a further 2 minutes.

3 Add half of the sliced chillies, the coconut milk, fish stock and tamarind water. Turn the heat down and simmer for 10 minutes.

4 Turn the heat up and throw the mussels into the pan. Cover the pan with a tight-fitting lid and cook until they just start to open – about 3 minutes. Add the rest of the chillies and the chopped coriander. Toss through, re-cover and heat for a further minute.

5 Once ready, season with a little salt and pepper and add lime juice to taste. Discard any unopened mussels. Serve in warmed bowls, with some good bread to mop up the delicious juices.

NOTE To make tamarind water, soak 1 tsp tamarind pulp in 1 tbsp hot water for 20 minutes, then press through a sieve to extract the infused liquid.

CLAMS AND COCKLES WITH CHERRY TOMATOES AND PANCETTA

This is a great way to enjoy fresh cockles and clams. If you cannot find fresh cockles, replace them with mussels... or use all mussels as a fresh-tasting alternative to cooking them in white wine and cream.

1kg fresh cockles

1kg fresh clams

50ml olive oil

150g pancetta (or smoked bacon), cubed

2 garlic cloves, peeled and crushed

pinch of dried chilli flakes

1 thyme sprig

200ml red wine

200ml fish stock (see page 247)

750g cherry tomatoes

salt and pepper

juice of ½ lemon, to taste

30g chopped parsley (preferably flat leaf)

4 SERVINGS

1   Wash the cockles and clams well under cold running water, discarding any with open or crushed shells. Drain and set aside.

2   Heat the olive oil in a pan (large enough to take all the ingredients) until just smoking. Add the pancetta and fry for about 5–6 minutes until just golden brown (or slightly crispy if you prefer).

3   Lower the heat slightly and add the garlic, chilli flakes and thyme. Cook for 2 minutes to release their flavours and aromas. Pour in the red wine and reduce down to a syrupy consistency. Add the fish stock and let bubble until reduced by half.

4   Next, add the tomatoes and cook for 8–10 minutes until they start to break down.

5   Increase the heat and add the cockles and clams. Stir well, cover with a tight-fitting lid and cook for 3–4 minutes or until the shells start to open. Toss well and add seasoning and lemon juice to taste (you may not need any salt). Discard any clams and cockles with unopened shells.

6   Once ready, add the chopped parsley, toss well together and divide among warmed bowls. Serve immediately.

CLAMS LINGUINI

2kg fresh clams, such as
 carpet shell or venus,
 cleaned

7 tbsp olive oil, plus extra
 to sprinkle

60g dried white
 breadcrumbs

2 shallots, peeled and
 finely chopped

½ leek, washed and
 finely chopped

1 carrot, peeled and finely
 chopped

1 celery stick, finely
 chopped

1 thyme sprig

2 flat leaf parsley sprigs

1 tsp black peppercorns,
 cracked

3 garlic cloves, peeled and
 finely chopped

75ml dry white wine

275g dried linguini (or fine
 spaghetti)

salt and pepper

6 tomatoes, skinned,
 deseeded and roughly
 chopped

small pinch of dried red
 chilli flakes

4 tbsp chopped flat leaf
 parsley

4 SERVINGS

1   Set the cleaned clams aside, discarding any that are open and don't close when tapped. Heat 2 tbsp olive oil in a frying pan and fry the breadcrumbs until golden and crispy. Remove and set aside.

2   Heat 3 tbsp olive oil in a large pan (with a tight-fitting lid) and fry the vegetables, herbs, peppercorns and one-third of the garlic until softened. Pour in the wine, bring to the boil and tip in the clams. Cover tightly and cook for 5 minutes or until the clams have opened, shaking the pan often.

3   Meanwhile, cook the pasta in a large pan of well salted boiling water for about 9 minutes until al dente.

4   When the clams are ready, drain in a colander set over a bowl to save the juices, discarding any that remain closed. Shell most of the clams, leaving about 24 in the shell, and set aside. Strain the reserved juices through a muslin-lined sieve to remove any grit.

5   For the sauce, heat 2 tbsp olive oil in a large frying pan and gently cook the remaining garlic for 2 minutes. Add the tomatoes, chilli flakes and reserved clam cooking juices. Increase the heat and reduce by half.

6   When the pasta is ready, drain and sprinkle with a little olive oil. Add to the reduced sauce and toss over the heat. Stir in the parsley, breadcrumbs and shelled clams and season to taste. Serve in warmed bowls, arranging the clams in shell around the edge.

TO PREPARE SCALLOPS

First you need to remove the scallops from their shells (unless your fishmonger has done this for you). Insert a sturdy knife in between the shells close to the hinge and prise them open. Remove the top shell. Cut through the muscle that attaches the meat to the lower shell and carefully slide the knife blade under the scallop to loosen it. Take it out and trim away the inedible fringe and dark muscle, leaving the white scallop muscle and coral (or roe). Carefully remove the coral, which is orange at the pointed end and creamy white at the end joining the muscle (unless you prefer to cook the scallops with their corals.)

SCALLOP POWDER

This is a wonderful way to preserve the delicate flavour of scallop coral. I use it as a seasoning to improve the flavour of all kinds of seafood dishes. It is well worth making some whenever you are serving a scallop dish, as it keeps well. You will need the corals from about 25 scallops to make a reasonable quantity. Cut away most of the creamy part of the corals and discard. If the corals are plump, cut them in half horizontally to speed up the drying process. Place the corals on a tray lined with silicone paper, spacing them apart. Leave to dry in a warm place, such as an airing cupboard (or a switched-off gas oven with the pilot light on) for several days, turning the scallops often to expose the soft parts to the warm, dry air. When the corals are dried out and brittle, place them in a food processor and blitz to a fine powder. Pass through a fine sieve and store in an airtight jar. Keep in a cool, dark cupboard and use as required. Sprinkle scallop powder over fish and shellfish dishes to enhance the taste. Even delicate fish such as John Dory are not overpowered by the subtle flavour.

SCALLOPS WITH GINGER SAUCE

18 medium fresh scallops,
  shelled and cleaned
lemon juice, to taste
salt and pepper
1 tsp olive oil

GINGER SAUCE

1 carrot, peeled
1 small onion, peeled
1 celery stick
1 small fennel bulb
60g fresh root ginger,
  peeled
2 tbsp virgin olive oil
5 garlic cloves, sliced
15 white peppercorns
2 star anise
1 tarragon sprig
1 thyme sprig
1 bay leaf
35ml white wine vinegar
70ml dry white wine
175ml each chicken and
  fish stock (page 247)
2 slices preserved stem
  ginger in syrup, drained
140ml butter sauce
  (see page 249)

SALAD GARNISH

handful of rocket leaves
handful of frisée
1 tbsp tarragon vinaigrette
  (see page 250)

6 SERVINGS

1　First make the ginger sauce. Cut the carrot, onion, celery, fennel and ginger into 5mm dice (cutting them finely helps to draw out their flavours during cooking). Heat the olive oil in a heavy-based pan over a low heat. Add the diced ginger and vegetables and sauté evenly for 5–10 minutes, without colouring. Add the garlic, peppercorns, star anise and herbs and cook, stirring, for another minute.

2　Pour the wine vinegar over the vegetables and let bubble until it has reduced to a sticky glaze, then add the wine and reduce this also to a sticky glaze.

3　Pour in both stocks and bring to the boil. Reduce the heat and simmer very gently for about 40 minutes until the liquor has reduced by two-thirds, skimming the surface from time to time. Remove the pan from the heat and pass the sauce through a fine sieve into a clean pan.

4　Allow the sauce to bubble slowly until it has reduced by half. Meanwhile, cut the stem ginger into fine julienne. Warm the butter sauce and whisk it into the ginger sauce. Add the ginger julienne and flavour with lemon juice and salt to taste. Keep warm.

5　For the garnish, toss the salad leaves in the vinaigrette. Arrange a pile of leaves on each serving plate.

6　To cook the scallops, heat a large heavy-based sauté pan over a high heat until it is very hot. Add the 1 tsp olive oil and tilt the pan to coat the whole surface with oil.

7　Place each scallop in the pan and cook without moving for 1–1½ minutes. Turn each scallop over (in the same order you put them into the pan to ensure even cooking) and cook on the other side for 1–1½ minutes until golden brown. Take off the heat and season with salt and pepper and a few drops of lemon juice.

8　Spoon some of the warm ginger sauce on to each plate and arrange the pan-fried scallops on top. Serve at once.

LOBSTER, CRAB & PRAWNS

Fresh lobsters are available all year, but are most abundant during the summer months. They can only be caught in special lobster pots, which is laborious and accounts for their high price, but they are a delicacy. A live lobster is dark blue or greenish in colour, depending on its habitat. The process of cooking turns the shell to its distinctive bright red colour.

Some of the best meat is found in the claws, so never buy a lobster with one missing. Pick lobsters that feel heavy for their size – those in captivity can get quite thin. A cock lobster will have meatier claws and firmer flesh, though in my view, a female lobster has a more delicate flavour. Large lobsters should only be used in terrines or for making mousseline (to fill pasta, etc.), as the meat is often tough. My favourite way to eat lobster is grilled, with a herb and anchovy butter.

Fresh crab is another treat. Fortunately, I'm able to buy crabs fresh from the day boats in Dartmouth. I think cock crabs have the best meat – hen meat tends to be a bit stringy and doesn't have as much flavour. Choose crabs that smell sweet and fresh, and again feel heavy for their size. I love eating crab – or fresh king prawns for that matter – with freshly baked bread and some good mayonnaise.

Cook live crabs and lobsters in a court bouillon (see page 247). Bring the liquid to the boil in a large cooking pot, drop in the crustacean(s) and return to the boil. Allow 8–10 minutes per 500g at a steady simmer. Once cooked, remove and leave to cool before extracting the meat.

SPICED PRAWNS AND STIR-FRIED VEGETABLES

This is a recipe that you're sure to go back to time and time again. Buy prawns with their shells on as this helps to maintain their succulent flavour.

400g raw tiger prawns

2 lemon grass stalks,
    outer leaves removed

1cm piece fresh root
    ginger, peeled

5 garlic cloves, peeled and
    chopped

1/2 red pepper, deseeded
    and roughly chopped

1/2 tsp ground turmeric

3/4 tsp salt

3 tbsp sunflower oil

2 tsp ground almonds

juice of 1 lime

STIR-FRIED VEGETABLES

3 tbsp sunflower oil

2 garlic cloves, peeled and
    thinly sliced

1cm piece fresh root
    ginger, peeled and cut
    into slivers

100g mangetout, trimmed

1 red pepper, deseeded
    and cut into strips

1 large courgette, cut into
    5cm long batons

15 basil leaves

75g mizuna leaves

soy sauce, to drizzle

SERVES 4

1   To prepare the prawns, pull off the head and legs and peel away the shell. Make a small slit along the back and remove the dark vein with the point of the knife. Rinse the prawns, pat dry and set aside.

2   Slice the lemon grass into thin rounds and place in a food processor along with the ginger, garlic, red pepper, turmeric and salt. Blend to a smooth paste, adding a little water if it seems too thick.

3   Heat the sunflower oil in a large frying pan. When it is hot, add the paste and fry for a minute or so until thickened. Add the prawns and give them a good stir. Now stir in the ground almonds, lime juice and 1½ tbsp water. Turn the heat up fairly high and sauté until the prawns are well coated in the paste and cooked through, about 5–6 minutes. Remove from the pan with a slotted spoon, leaving behind the oil, and place on a warmed plate. Keep warm while you stir-fry the vegetables.

4   Heat the sunflower oil in a wok over a high heat. When it just starts to smoke, throw in the garlic and ginger and toss quickly until golden. Add the mangetout and stir-fry for about 20 seconds. Now add the red pepper and courgette and toss quickly over the high heat for about 2 minutes.

5   Now throw in the basil and mizuna leaves and continue to stir-fry for 30 seconds. Pile into the centre of warmed plates, drizzle over a little soy sauce and spoon the prawns on top. Serve with plain boiled rice.

CRAB (OR LOBSTER) BISQUE

Packed with flavour, this wonderful soup makes a great light lunch if you serve some good crusty bread alongside. I also use this bisque as a sauce for a number of fish dishes. The more you reduce the finished sauce, the more concentrated the flavour.

2kg crab (or lobster) bones

100ml olive oil

50g unsalted butter

1 large onion, peeled and chopped

1 large leek, washed and chopped

2 celery sticks, chopped

1/2 fennel bulb, chopped

10g garlic cloves, peeled and finely chopped

100g tomato purée

6 plum tomatoes, chopped and deseeded

200ml dry white wine

150ml Noilly Prat (or other dry vermouth)

2 litres fish stock (see page 247)

1 bay leaf

2 thyme sprigs

1 tarragon sprig, blanched (briefly in boiling water)

100ml double cream

salt and pepper

juice of 1/2 lemon, or to taste

6–8 SERVINGS

1   Chop the crab (or lobster) bones into small pieces. Place a large pan (that will hold everything) over a high heat. When it is hot, add the olive oil and heat until it is almost smoking. Add the chopped bones and cook until they are golden and slightly caramelised. This will take around 10–15 minutes.

2   Add the butter, chopped vegetables and garlic and cook for a further 10 minutes or until the vegetables are softened and starting to colour.

3   Add the tomato purée and tomatoes. Stir well and cook for a further 5–7 minutes to release the flavour from the purée and reduce the acidity of the tomatoes.

4   Add the wine and let bubble until totally reduced. Add the vermouth and reduce by at least half. Pour in the stock, bring back to the boil and skim. Add the herbs, lower the heat and allow to simmer gently for 1 1/2–2 hours. Take off the heat and cool slightly.

5   Blitz the soup in a blender, in batches as necessary, to release more flavour from the bones. Pass the soup through a fine sieve into a clean pan, pushing the residue in the sieve with the back of a ladle to extract as much juice and flavour as possible.

6   Stir the cream into the soup, bring back to a simmer and reduce slightly to thicken. Check the seasoning – you will probably need to add a little salt and pepper and a squeeze of lemon juice. Once ready, serve.

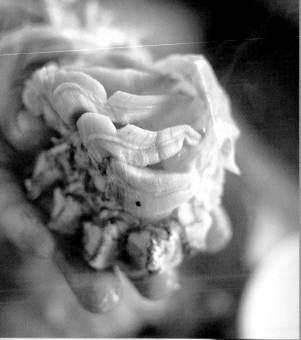

PREPARING A CRAB

This is easier than it appears to be and well worth the effort, because fresh crab meat tastes sublime. After cooking, when the crab is cool enough to handle, twist off the claws and legs, then separate the body from the main shell. To do this, insert a knife in between the shells and twist to separate them, then push the body up firmly with your hands until it comes away from the main shell. Remove the inedible dead man's fingers from the body – easily recognised from the photograph (above left).

Loosen the brown meat in the main shell and spoon into a bowl. Prise out the white meat from the body section with a fine skewer or lobster pick and keep it separate from the brown meat. Also, use the skewer to extract the white meat from the legs. Crack the large claws open with a mallet or rolling pin and carefully ease out the white meat – this is the best bit! Check the meat for any fragments of shell. The crab meat is then ready to eat.

STEAMED CRAB PARCELS WITH CRAB BISQUE

This simple dish is a great way to savour beautiful fresh crab. The delicate white meat and some of the dark meat is used to make elegant little parcels, which are served on a pool of fragrant bisque, prepared from the shells. Nothing is thrown away.

20g young spinach leaves, washed and patted dry

300g white crab meat

10g brown crab meat

10g flaked almonds, toasted and coarsely chopped

10g cured ham, chopped

30g red pepper

salt and pepper

1 tsp groundnut oil

1 tsp white wine vinegar

juice of ½ lemon, or to taste

pinch of cayenne pepper

1 Iceberg lettuce (outer leaves only)

TO SERVE:

1 quantity Crab Bisque (see page 99)

coriander sprigs, to garnish

4 SERVINGS

1   Finely chop the spinach and put into a bowl with the white and brown crab meat. Add the nuts and ham and fork through.

2   Using a peeler, skin the red pepper, then blanch in boiling salted water for 2 minutes. Refresh in cold water, drain and dice finely. Heat the oil in a frying pan, add the red pepper and a little seasoning and fry quickly for 2 minutes. Add the wine vinegar and cook until evaporated. Leave to cool.

3   Add the red pepper to the crab with a squeeze of lemon juice (don't make it too acidic). Sprinkle in the cayenne and check the seasoning.

4   Bring a large pan of salted water to the boil. One by one, blanch the lettuce leaves in the boiling water for 30 seconds. Remove with a slotted spoon and refresh in iced water. Drain carefully and pat the leaves dry with a tea towel. If the stalk end is still crispy, remove it with a knife.

5   Lay 4 lettuce leaves out on a clean surface. Divide the crab mix into 4 portions and roll into balls. Place one in the centre of each leaf and gently wrap it in the leaf. Press each parcel in your hand to ensure it is sealed and a good shape.

6   Heat the water in your steamer and put the crab parcels in the basket. Cover and steam for 8 minutes. Meanwhile, reheat the crab bisque if necessary.

7   Put the parcels in the centre of warmed soup plates and ladle the bisque around. Garnish with coriander and serve.

SQUID & CUTTLEFISH

Squid is popular all around the Med. My kids love it and we ate it a lot when we lived in southwest France. It is considered a delicacy in Spain, indeed 75 per cent of the squid and cuttlefish caught around our shores goes over to Spain. In Mediterranean countries, fisherman catch squid at night, shining a bright light into the water. The squid are attracted to this light and will gather in great numbers ready to be scooped up in the fishermen's nets. In some countries the ink is used to colour and lightly flavour the dish, as in the Italian risotto nero (black rice). You can substitute cuttlefish in any squid dish, though cuttlefish are usually tougher and take longer to cook.

Squid are sold whole or cleaned. Small squid are likely to be more tender and have a sweeter flavour, though larger ones can be improved by marinating before cooking. The freshness of squid is all-important. The body (once the membrane has been removed) should be pearly white. If it is turning pink, it is not as fresh as it should be. Also the odour should be mild. Basically, if it's pink and stinks don't buy it! Never overcook squid, or it will be rubbery.

To prepare squid, pull the head from the body firmly to separate the tentacles and remove the innards; retain the ink sac if you wish to use it. Peel off the skin from the pouch and pull out the quill. Squeeze out the beak from the tentacles, then cut the tentacles away from the head. Rinse the pouch and tentacles under cold running water. Unless stuffing them whole, slice pouches before cooking. Larger squid pouches can be opened out and scored to help tenderise the flesh.

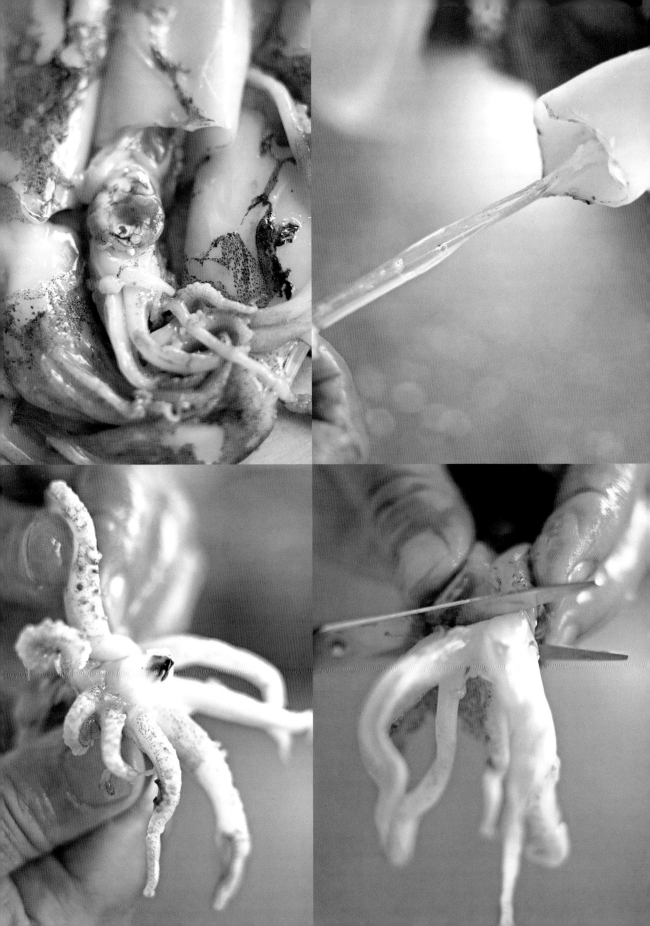

TEMPURA OF SQUID WITH A MINTED MAYONNAISE

I love the contrast of a fresh-tasting herby mayonnaise with crispy squid, but you can serve it with a sweet chilli jam if you prefer.

500g fresh baby squid

salt and pepper

cayenne pepper

sunflower oil, for
    deep-frying

flour, for dusting

lemon juice, to taste

BATTER

45g plain flour

30g cornflour

15g baking powder

125ml sparkling water,
    chilled

4 ice cubes

MINTED MAYONNAISE

150ml mayonnaise (see
    page 250)

15g mint leaves, chopped

pinch of cayenne pepper

squeeze of lemon juice

GARNISH

50g rocket leaves

50ml tarragon vinaigrette
    (see page 250)

4 SERVINGS

1   First prepare the mayonnaise (you can do this the day before to allow the mayo to take on more of the mint flavour if you like). Mix the chopped mint into the mayonnaise and add salt, cayenne pepper and a little lemon juice to taste.

2   Prepare the squid (see page 104), keeping the tentacles, but discarding the ink sac. Rinse well under cold running water. Cut the pouches into 1cm thick rings, pat dry on kitchen paper and set aside with the tentacles.

3   For the batter, combine the flour, cornflour and baking powder in a bowl and add a pinch each of salt and cayenne pepper. Slowly add the sparkling water, mixing the batter with a spoon or chopstick. Don't worry if there are a few lumps – this is normal for tempura batter. Finally add the ice cubes and keep in the fridge until ready to use.

4   When you are ready to eat the squid, dress the rocket leaves with the tarragon vinaigrette.

5   In a suitable pan for deep-frying, heat the sunflower oil to about 180°C. Dust a handful of squid with seasoned flour, dip into the batter to coat, then immerse in the hot oil. Fry until the pieces rise to the surface and float, indicating that they are ready – this only takes a minute or two. Don't overcook the squid otherwise it will be tough and rubbery. Remove and drain on kitchen paper. Repeat until all the squid is cooked.

6   Season the squid with salt and pepper and squeeze over a little lemon juice. Divide among plates and garnish with the rocket salad. Place a spoonful of minted mayonnaise alongside and serve immediately.

GRILLED STUFFED SQUID WITH BRAISED TOMATO SAUCE AND BASIL

You don't need the squid tentacles for this dish, but you could always cook them in tempura batter and serve them as an appetiser with drinks (see page 106).

12–16 fresh baby squid
   pouches, cleaned (see
   page 104)
juice of ¼ lemon, to taste
20ml unsalted butter,
   melted
salt and pepper

SCALLOP STUFFING

4 large fresh scallops,
   cleaned and corals
   removed
1 tarragon sprig, blanched
   (briefly in boiling water)
1 egg
salt
cayenne pepper
20ml whipping cream
squeeze of lemon juice,
   to taste

TO SERVE

150ml braised tomato
   sauce (see page 248)
1 tbsp finely shredded
   basil leaves (optional)
deep-fried parsley sprigs
   (optional)

6 SERVINGS

1   Make sure all of the outer skin has been removed from the squid pouches and check that they are thoroughly cleaned inside. Wash under cold running water and pat dry on kitchen paper.

2   Next, prepare the stuffing. Tip the scallops into a blender and whiz until smooth. Add the blanched tarragon and egg and blend again until smooth. Now add a pinch each of salt and cayenne pepper with the cream. Blend until you have a velvety smooth mousseline. Transfer to a bowl and flavour with a little lemon juice to taste. Cover and chill in the fridge for 20 minutes.

3   Once chilled, spoon the scallop mousseline into a piping bag fitted with a large plain nozzle and use to fill the squid pouches.

4   Preheat the grill to high. Reheat the braised tomato sauce, add a little shredded basil if you like and check the seasoning. Keep hot.

5   Place the stuffed squid pouches on a sturdy baking tray and brush them with a little lemon juice and melted butter. Season with salt and pepper.

6   Place under the hot grill and cook for about 3 minutes on one side. Turn over and cook for a further 2½–3 minutes. Remove from the heat and squeeze over a little lemon juice.

7   To serve, place a large spoonful of tomato sauce in the centre of each warmed plate and arrange the squid pouches on top. Garnish with deep-fried parsley sprigs if you wish and serve immediately. Egg tagliatelle is good with this dish. I also like to serve a green salad on the side.

COD, HADDOCK & HAKE

Cod is available all year, although it is at its best during the winter months. However due to years of overfishing, drastic measures are needed to help restore dwindling numbers around our coastline. The same applies to haddock and hake, so we need to consider alternative fish, which have a comparable texture and flavour. You can use cod, haddock or hake (preferably from sustainable stocks) or any chunky white fish for the recipes in this section – even large pollack caught off the beach and cooked the same evening.

Haddock is easily distinguishable from cod by the black lateral line running down its back and its slightly larger eyes. I'm very partial to hake. It tends to be a bit more expensive, but has lighter flesh than cod or haddock and is suited to more delicate dishes. Another benefit is that it has few bones and even these are easy to remove.

With all three fish, go for cuts from the middle as these bring together the fuller flavour of the shoulder and the tenderness of the tail. Preparation is fairly straightforward and it is usual for the fishmonger to fillet the fish for you. Avoid fillets that have yellow or pink patches as these indicate a dubious quality.

As far as cooking is concerned, these fish are versatile. Large fillets are great coated with a herb crust, oven-roasted and served with a sprinkle of lemon juice. They are also good for making fish cakes, which I serve with a parsley or hollandaise sauce. Most other methods applied to fish are suitable, although I wouldn't advise poaching cod unless it is extremely fresh as it would probably have little flavour.

BAKED HAKE WITH SMOKED SALMON AND A HERB BUTTER

Enveloping hake in smoked salmon and serving it with a herb butter sauce really enhances its flavour. If you can't get hake, use cod, haddock or any other chunky white fish.

4 thick filleted hake portions, about 150g each
400g smoked salmon
50ml olive oil
50g unsalted butter, in pieces
salt and pepper
juice of ½ lemon, or to taste

HERB BUTTER SAUCE
500ml fish stock (see page 247)
1 garlic clove, peeled
1 tarragon sprig, blanched (briefly in boiling water)
200g herb and anchovy butter (see page 249), diced
few drops of lemon juice (optional)

4 SERVINGS

1   Preheat the oven to 200°C/Gas 6. Check over the hake portions for bones. With a sharp knife, cut the smoked salmon into long wide strips, the same width as the hake pieces. Wrap the hake portions in the smoked salmon and secure with cocktail sticks. Cover and refrigerate until ready to cook.

2   For the herb butter sauce, pour the stock into a pan, add the garlic clove and blanched tarragon and bring to the boil over a high heat. Skim and let bubble until reduced by half. Strain the stock into a clean pan.

3   Gradually whisk the diced herb butter into the reduced stock. When it is all incorporated, the sauce should be thick enough to coat the back of a spoon. Check the seasoning and add a little lemon juice to sharpen the taste if you need to. Keep warm until ready to serve.

4   To cook the hake, place a large non-stick ovenproof frying pan over a medium-high heat, add the olive oil and heat until almost smoking. Place the hake parcels in the pan, turn the heat down slightly and cook for 2–3 minutes. Turn the hake parcels over and dot with the unsalted butter. Place in the oven and cook for a further 5–6 minutes until the fish is ready.

5   Meanwhile, gently reheat the herb butter sauce, but don't let it boil or it will split. Transfer the hake parcels to warmed plates, grind over some pepper and sprinkle with a little lemon juice. Serve with new potatoes and asparagus.

ROASTED HADDOCK IN A MUSTARD AND CHIVE SAUCE

I serve this dish at The New Angel, gently smoking the haddock over applewood chips before cooking. I don't advise you to do this at home though, as it makes a hell of a mess! The dish is still very good with fresh, unsmoked haddock. It makes a great lunch with crusty bread.

4 portions of filleted haddock, cut from the thick end, about 200g each, skinned

300g French beans or sugar snap peas, trimmed

salt and pepper

20ml olive oil

4 free-range duck eggs (or large hen's eggs)

2 tsp malt vinegar or white wine vinegar

30g unsalted butter

juice of ½ lemon, or to taste

MUSTARD AND CHIVE SAUCE

150ml warm butter sauce (see page 249)

2 tsp wholegrain mustard

20g chives, chopped

4 SERVINGS

1   Preheat the oven to 180°C/Gas 4. Check the haddock portions for small bones.

2   Cook the French beans or sugar snaps in boiling salted water for 3–4 minutes until just tender, but retaining a slight bite. Drain and refresh in iced water, then drain again and set aside.

3   Next, prepare the sauce. Flavour the warm butter sauce with the mustard and chives. Taste and adjust the seasoning. Keep warm until ready to serve.

4   Place a large non-stick ovenproof frying pan over a high heat and add the olive oil. When almost smoking, add the haddock pieces and season with salt and pepper. Cook for about 3 minutes, without moving the pieces, until golden brown underneath. Turn the haddock pieces over and finish cooking in the oven for about 5–6 minutes.

5   Meanwhile, poach the eggs. Bring a wide, shallow pan of lightly salted water to the boil, with the vinegar added. Stir the water using a brisk circular motion, then crack the eggs into the water. (The movement helps the eggs to set in a neat shape.) Poach for 3–4 minutes or until the yolks are just soft and the whites are slightly firm to the touch. As soon as they are ready, remove with a slotted spoon.

6   While the eggs are poaching, reheat the beans or sugar snaps in the butter and season with salt and pepper to taste. This will only take a couple of minutes.

7   As soon as the haddock is cooked, remove from the oven and squeeze over a little lemon juice. Spoon a portion of beans or peas in the centre of each warmed plate and lay a haddock portion on top. Place a poached egg on top, spoon over the mustard and chive sauce and serve.

COD EN PAPILLOTE WITH BOULANGERE POTATOES

The aroma that emerges from these parcels as you open them is truly amazing. You can use any combination of mushrooms – girolles, blewits, morels, enochi, crimini and chestnut mushrooms are all suitable. Serve with a simple accompaniment, such as wilted spinach.

4 portions of filleted cod, cut from the thick end, about 150g each, skinned

900ml chicken stock (see page 247)

600g floury potatoes, such as King Edward, peeled

1 small onion, peeled and thinly sliced

4 tbsp thyme leaves, chopped

salt and pepper

100g clarified butter (see page 251)

250g mixed wild and cultivated mushrooms, cleaned, sliced if large

1/2 garlic clove, peeled and finely chopped

50g unsalted butter

truffle oil (optional), to serve

4 SERVINGS

1   Preheat the oven to 200°C/Gas 6. Check over the cod for pin bones. For the parcels, cut 4 pieces of greaseproof paper and 4 pieces of foil, each measuring 45 x 60cm.

2   Bring the stock to the boil in a large pan and reduce by half. Cut the potatoes into 5mm thick slices. Add to the stock with the onion, half the thyme and some seasoning. Bring back to the boil and cook for 5–7 minutes until the potatoes are just tender but still holding their shape.

3   Season the cod fillets. Heat 3 tbsp clarified butter in a large frying pan and fry the cod, skin side down, for about 3 minutes until the skin is an appetising brown colour. Remove from the pan using a fish slice and set aside.

4   Heat the remaining clarified butter in the pan, then add the mushrooms, garlic and some seasoning. Fry, stirring, for 3 minutes until golden. Remove and set aside.

5   To make the parcels, lay one piece of greaseproof paper on the work surface and place a sheet of foil on top, with a longer edge facing you. Arrange a quarter of the potato slices on the foil slightly off centre, overlapping them to form a bed. Place a cod fillet, skin side up, on top and scatter the mushrooms over. Put a couple of knobs of butter on top and sprinkle with a quarter of the remaining thyme.

6   Bring the far corners up to meet the near corners. Starting from the left corner and working all the way round to the other side, fold over 3cm of the paper and foil at a time. Repeat the process once more to ensure a good seal. The parcel will resemble a pasty. Repeat to make 3 more.

7   Place the parcels in the oven and cook for 12 minutes. Let your guests open the parcels at the table and hand round truffle oil to sprinkle over if you like.

SALMON & SEA TROUT

I'm not enamoured with farmed salmon. I know that there are some good salmon farms, but I have visited some awful ones, where fish are kept 20 deep in small netted areas and fed on pellets containing colourings and various antibiotics. I've seen salmon with damaged fins and salmon covered in ticks… I've even witnessed supermarket buyers being offered the equivalent of a paint colour chart to choose the colour of next season's salmon! Out of choice, unless I know where it's come from, I would never touch a farmed salmon.

On the other hand, there's nothing better than a lovely oily wild salmon or sea trout. Like salmon, sea trout feed in the sea, but return to the river to spawn. Wild salmon is at its best during spring and summer and has rich pink flesh. Sea trout is available all year round.

Fresh salmon and sea trout should be firm to the touch so avoid steaks that are soft or watery. When buying a whole salmon, choose one that is short and oval with broad shoulders and a small head. Both fish can be pan-fried, poached, baked or grilled. And finely sliced raw salmon, marinated with lemon and olive oil, makes a lovely carpaccio.

Filleting a whole fish isn't difficult. Scrape off the scales (if necessary) under cold running water from tail end to head. Then cut along the belly, remove the innards and gills and wash out the blood line along the backbone. To fillet the fish in two, extend the opening along the length of the fish and skim the knife over the bones to detach the fillet. Turn the fish over and repeat on the other side. Use tweezers to remove tiny 'pin' bones from the flesh and cut into portions if required.

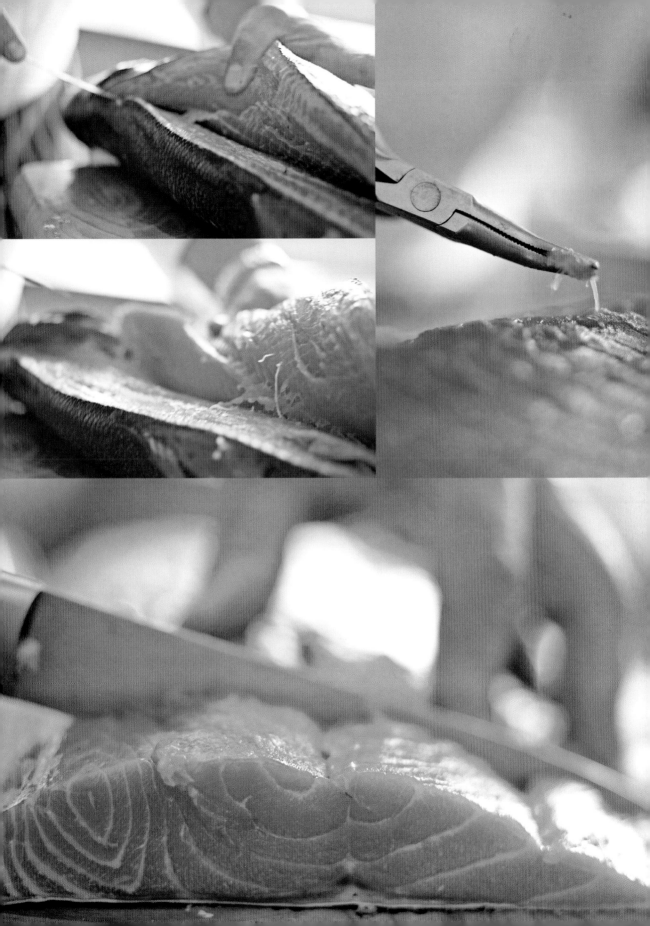

SEARED FILLET OF SALMON WITH LENTILS AND PISTOU

4 salmon fillets, with
   skin, about 200g each
salt and pepper
3 tbsp olive oil

LENTILS

150g Puy or Castelluccio
   lentils
700ml chicken stock (see
   page 247)
50g smoked bacon
   (preferably in one piece)
1 garlic clove, peeled and
   crushed
1 bay leaf
2 thyme sprigs
1/2 tsp salt
100g carrots, peeled and
   finely diced

PISTOU SAUCE

50g basil leaves blanched
   (briefly in boiling water)
1/2 tsp crushed garlic
150ml olive oil
2 tomatoes
1–2 tsp lemon juice, to
   taste

4 SERVINGS

1   First cook the lentils. Put them in a pan with the stock, smoked bacon, garlic, bay leaf and thyme and bring to the boil. Skim off any scum and reduce the heat to a simmer. Cook for 20–25 minutes or until the lentils are just tender, adding the salt and diced carrots halfway through cooking. Take off the heat and set to one side.

2   Next, make the pistou sauce. Whiz the blanched basil, garlic and olive oil in a blender or food processor until smooth, then pour into a bowl. Peel, halve and deseed the tomatoes, then cut into 5mm dice. Add to the sauce and season with salt and pepper to taste. Now add the lemon juice, a few drops at a time, tasting as you go.

3   Season the salmon fillets on both sides with salt and pepper. Place a large non-stick frying pan over a high heat and add the 3 tbsp olive oil. When it is almost smoking, lay the salmon fillets in the pan, skin side down and cook for 3 minutes. Turn the fillets over and cook for about 2 minutes for a perfect pink result.

4   To serve, remove the bacon from the lentils and discard. Next, reheat the lentils gently and check the seasoning. Place a spoonful of lentils in the centre of each warmed plate and lay a salmon fillet on top, skin side up. Drizzle the pistou over and around the salmon and serve. New potatoes – ideally Jersey Royals – tossed in a little butter are great with this dish.

BEETROOT MARINATED SALMON WITH HORSERADISH CREAM

Everyone knows about the beauty of horseradish with salmon or even smoked mackerel, but marinating the fish with grated beetroot, as I have here, may be rather less familiar. The beetroot cuts the richness of the salmon beautifully... a great partnership.

2kg side of filleted
   salmon
300g coarse salt
100g granulated sugar
finely pared zest and
   juice of 1 lemon
finely pared zest of
   1 orange
1 bunch of dill, chopped
500g beetroot, cooked
   and peeled

HORSERADISH CREAM
200ml whipping cream
55g fresh horseradish,
   freshly grated
½ bunch of chives,
   chopped
salt and pepper

6–8 SERVINGS

1 Skin the salmon fillet and check for pin bones. Make 8 shallow slits in the flesh – just deep enough for the marinade to penetrate. Lay the salmon on a sheet of cling film. Mix the salt and sugar together in a bowl. Cut the lemon and orange zests into very fine strips and add to the bowl with the lemon juice and dill; mix well. Spread this mixture on both sides of the salmon and wrap in the cling film. Lay in a shallow dish and leave to marinate overnight (maximum of 12 hours) in the fridge.

2 The next day, rinse the salt mix off under cold running water and pat the salmon dry on a cloth. Grate the cooked beetroot into a bowl, retaining all the juices.

3 Place the salmon in a roasting tray and spread the grated beetroot all over it. Cover with a sheet of cling film and place another roasting tray on top to press the beetroot into the salmon. Leave to marinate in the fridge for about 6–8 hours.

4 To make the horseradish cream, put the cream in a bowl and stir in the horseradish, then add the chives and season with salt and a little pepper. Pass through a sieve into a clean bowl and whip until thick. Refrigerate until ready to serve.

5 When the salmon is ready, there will be a deep purple colour running through it (from the beetroot). Scrape the grated beetroot off the fillet and reserve.

6 When ready to serve, slice the salmon into wafer-thin slices, using a sharp knife. Arrange on serving plates, to reveal the attractive beetroot staining. Dress each serving with a spoonful of grated beetroot and a dollop of horseradish cream. Serve with slices of brown bread.

CHARGRILLED SEA TROUT WITH A CITRUS MARINADE

This simple recipe also works for salmon, wild brown trout, even fish like snapper and red mullet. The sweet and sour flavours really brings out the taste of the fish.

4 sea trout fillets, about
   170g each
3 tbsp olive oil

MARINADE
300ml olive oil
5g coriander seeds,
   crushed
1 garlic clove, peeled and
   crushed
1 bay leaf, chopped
12 black peppercorns,
   crushed
2 finely pared strips of
   lemon zest, finely
   shredded
juice of 1 lemon
juice of 1 orange
juice of 1 lime
1 star anise, crushed
salt and pepper
pinch of sugar

TO GARNISH
flat leaf parsley or chervil
   sprigs

4 SERVINGS

1   Preheat the oven to 170°C/Gas 3. Check the fish fillets for any small bones, removing any you find with tweezers. Combine all the marinade ingredients in a bowl, seasoning with a little salt and pepper, plus the pinch of sugar to counteract the acidity. Mix well.

2   Lay the fish fillets in a suitable deep tray and pour the marinade over them. Turn to coat, then cover and leave to marinate for about 1½–2 hours, turning the fish regularly to allow the flavour of the marinade to penetrate the flesh. (You can leave it longer if you wish, but not too long, otherwise the acidity will cook the fish!) Remove the fish, reserving the marinade.

3   When ready to cook, heat an ovenproof griddle pan or large non-stick frying pan over a medium-high heat and then add the 3 tbsp olive oil. Once it is almost smoking, lay the fish fillets in the pan, skin side down, and cook for 2 minutes. Turn the fillets over and finish cooking in the oven for 6 minutes. Insert a sharp knife into the thickest part of the flesh to check that it is cooked.

4   Meanwhile, tip the marinade into a pan and warm through over a low heat. Don't allow it to reduce down as this would make the marinade too acidic and ruin the delicate flavour.

5   Once the fish is ready, transfer to warmed plates and pour over the warm marinade. Garnish with herbs and serve.

SEA BASS, RED MULLET, JOHN DORY & MONKFISH

Sea bass is highly prized in the fishing world and is one of my favourite fish. Shaped like a salmon, it is steely grey in colour, with a white belly. Here in Devon, sea bass are abundant for about 12 weeks from the end of May, when they swim up with the Gulf Stream. They have relatively few bones and a fine flavour. I love to simply grill or roast sea bass, but it is also delicious poached in wine or champagne.

Red mullet are distinguishable by their colour and delicate flesh. I've worked with French chefs who love to cook tiny ones – *rouget de roche* – but I prefer bigger fish, which have more fat and a deeper flesh colour. Line-caught red mullet are the best – those caught in a net are more likely to be battered and bruised. In cooking you can treat red mullet in the same way as sea bass, so recipes are interchangeable.

John Dory is a delicate fish with a firm and consistent flavour. The trouble is, like me it has a huge head! So bear in mind that if you buy a whole John Dory, after decapitation you will lose about 60 per cent. Cook it only until the flesh is just opaque. If you overcook this fish, throw it away, as the texture and flavour will be ruined.

If you saw a monkfish with its huge ugly head on you would probably avoid it at all costs, but the tail, which is the only part that is eaten, has wonderful firm, meaty white flesh. I treat large monkfish fillets in the same way as steaks – roasting or pan-frying them, then resting them for a while before serving. Smaller tails are delicious poached.

STEAMED SEA BASS FILLETS WITH BASIL BUTTER SAUCE

This is such an enticing dish. A vibrant spinach and basil butter sauce is the perfect foil for beautiful sea bass fillets, which I like to serve on a bed of cannellini beans flavoured with diced peppers and courgettes (see page 80).

600g sea bass fillet
salt and pepper
240ml fish stock (see
    page 247)
1 slice of garlic
1 tarragon sprig, blanched

BASIL BUTTER
1 bunch of basil, trimmed
100g leaf spinach, cleaned
120g unsalted butter, soft

GARNISH
deep-fried or fresh basil

4 SERVINGS

1   First prepare the basil butter. Blanch the basil and spinach leaves briefly by immersing them in boiling water for a few seconds, then drain and pat dry with kitchen paper. Tip the leaves into a blender and whiz to chop finely, then add the butter and blend until completely smooth and velvety. The butter will turn bright green. Transfer to a small bowl, cover and refrigerate until later.

2   Preheat the oven to 180°C/Gas 4. Cut the sea bass into 4 equal portions, check for pin bones and season with salt and pepper. Pour two-thirds of the stock into a shallow ovenproof sauté pan, add the garlic and tarragon and bring to the boil.

3   Lay the fish fillets in the pan and lower the heat. Place a piece of buttered greaseproof paper over the fish and cover with a tight-fitting lid. Transfer the pan to the oven to steam the fish for 5–7 minutes until just cooked. (Meanwhile, warm the cannellini beans in the remaining stock in another pan and check the seasoning.)

4   Lift the fish fillets on to a warmed plate and keep warm. Return the sauté pan to the hob over a medium heat and reduce the stock by half, then lower the heat. Slowly add the basil butter, a piece at a time, whisking constantly – the sauce will thicken as you do so. (Don't let it boil, or the sauce will split.) Once all the butter is incorporated, strain the sauce through a sieve into a warm jug and season with salt and pepper.

5   Serve each portion of sea bass, skin side up, on a bed of cannellini beans with peppers and courgettes. Pour the basil butter sauce around and garnish with deep-fried (or fresh) basil leaves. Serve immediately.

WARM SALAD OF JOHN DORY, ORANGE AND AVOCADO

John Dory is a superb fish with a delicate flavour and melting texture. A fresh-tasting salad is the ideal complement. If you get the fishmonger to fillet the fish for you, ask for the bones and heads as these are excellent for making stock.

2 John Dory, about 550g
    each
olive oil, for cooking
salt and pepper

SALAD

1 orange, plus the juice of
    another orange
pinch of sugar
1 tbsp white wine vinegar
1 tbsp olive oil
½ curly endive, roughly
    torn
2 plum tomatoes, peeled,
    deseeded and diced
1 ripe avocado
30g pine nuts, lightly
    toasted

4 SERVINGS

1   Fillet and skin the John Dory, or get your fishmonger to do this for you. Cut each fillet into three along its natural dividing lines. Cut the larger strip from each fish in two, to give 16 fillet strips in total. Check for any pin bones.

2   For the salad, peel and segment the orange and place in a bowl; set aside. Squeeze the juice from the orange shell into a pan and add the juice from the other orange. Bring to the boil, then skim and lower the heat. Simmer to reduce to 2 tbsp. Transfer to another bowl and let cool, then whisk in the sugar, wine vinegar and olive oil to make the dressing. Season with salt and pepper and set aside.

3   Break up the endive leaves, rinse and pat dry. Place them in a large bowl with the orange segments and tomatoes. Halve, stone, peel and dice the avocado and add to the salad with the toasted pine nuts and dressing. Toss to mix and check the seasoning.

4   Place a heavy-based frying pan over a high heat and add a little oil. Season the John Dory fillets with salt and pepper. When the oil is almost smoking, gently place the fillets in the pan and cook them quickly for only 30 seconds on each side. (As John Dory is a delicate fish, it is important to avoid overcooking it.) Remove the fillets from the pan and drain on kitchen paper.

5   To serve, pile the salad into the centre of warmed plates and carefully arrange the pieces of warm fish on top. Drizzle over any remaining dressing and serve at once.

JOHN DORY WITH ASPARAGUS AND GRIBICHE SAUCE

It is important to partner John Dory with ingredients that won't overpower its beautiful, subtle flavour. Homegrown asparagus fits with this concept, but if you can't get any, use extra fine French beans or new season's baby leeks instead.

2 John Dory, about 550g
   each
12 asparagus spears,
   trimmed
salt and pepper
olive oil, for cooking

GRIBICHE SAUCE
2 large eggs
1 tsp red wine vinegar
2 tsp Dijon mustard
175ml groundnut or
   sunflower oil (or a
   mixture)
1 tbsp capers, finely
   chopped
1 shallot, peeled and
   finely chopped
3 gherkins, finely
   chopped
2 tarragon sprigs, finely
   chopped
1 tbsp flat leaf parsley,
   finely chopped

4 SERVINGS

1   Fillet and skin the John Dory, or get your fishmonger to do this for you. Cut each fillet into three along its natural dividing lines. Cut the larger strip from each fish in two, to give 16 fillet strips in total. Check for any pin bones.

2   Blanch the asparagus spears in a pan of boiling salted water for 1 minute, then drain and refresh in cold water. Drain again and set aside.

3   For the gribiche sauce, boil the eggs for 5 minutes, then drain and cool quickly under cold running water. Peel and halve, then scoop out the soft yolks into a bowl, reserving the set whites. Add the wine vinegar, mustard and some salt and pepper to the yolks and whisk to combine. Slowly pour in the oil in a steady stream, whisking all the time until you have the consistency of a mayonnaise. Dice the egg white and add to the sauce, along with all the other ingredients. Stir to mix, then set aside.

4   Heat a griddle pan over a medium-high heat. Roll the asparagus spears in salt, pepper and olive oil to coat, then place in the griddle pan. Cook, turning occasionally, until nicely charred all over. At the same time, heat up a large frying pan and oil lightly. Season the John Dory fillets and cook them quickly for just 30 seconds on each side. Remove and drain on kitchen paper.

5   Lay the asparagus spears in the centre of warmed plates and top with the John Dory fillets. Spoon the sauce on top and serve straight away.

RED MULLET WITH OLIVE AND ANCHOVY ROASTED POTATOES

Red mullet is one of the tastiest of all fish and, with its silvery pink skin, it's certainly one of the prettiest. If you are only able to find small fillets, then allow two per person. If you are buying whole fish and preparing them yourself, don't discard the liver – it is a real delicacy. Instead, flash-fry in a little clarified butter and serve on garlic croûtes... delicious.

900g floury potatoes, such as King Edward or Maris Piper, peeled

salt and pepper

5 tbsp olive oil

2 tender rosemary sprigs, leaves stripped and roughly chopped

10 Kalamata olives, pitted and sliced lengthways

2 tbsp small capers

4 semi-dried tomatoes, sliced

4 anchovy fillets, halved lengthways

4 red mullet fillets, about 160–180g each

2 tbsp flat leaf parsley, roughly chopped

4 SERVINGS

1   Preheat the oven to 200°C/Gas 6. Halve the potatoes lengthways, then cut into wedges. Place in a pan of lightly salted water and par-boil for 5–7 minutes. Do not overcook at this stage – the potatoes need to hold their shape.

2   Drain the potatoes well and place on a shallow baking tray. Drizzle with most of the olive oil, toss to coat and season with plenty of pepper. Roast in the oven for about 50 minutes, turning halfway through cooking.

3   When the potato wedges are golden brown, take out of the oven and add the rosemary, olives, capers, semi-dried tomatoes and anchovy strips. Mix well and return to the oven for 8–10 minutes.

4   Meanwhile, check the red mullet fillets for pin bones and heat up a griddle pan. Brush the fish with olive oil and season with salt and pepper. Lay the fillets skin side down on the griddle and cook for 3 minutes or until the skin releases itself from the griddle pan. Turn over and cook for a further minute.

5   Once cooked, remove the fish fillets to a warmed plate. To serve, toss the parsley through the potatoes and spoon them into the centre of warmed plates. Place the red mullet fillets on top and serve immediately.

GRILLED RED MULLET WITH COUSCOUS AND CHARMOULA

4–6 red mullet fillets,
   about 160g each

CHARMOULA
bunch of coriander, leaves
   only, chopped
1 red chilli, deseeded and
   chopped
1 tsp chopped garlic
2 tbsp mint leaves
2 pinches of ground
   cumin
1 tsp ground coriander
pinch of saffron strands
175ml olive oil

COUSCOUS SALAD
1 red pepper
1 tsp tomato purée
1 tsp red wine vinegar
1½ tsp olive oil
150g couscous
250ml chicken stock (see
   page 247)
3 vine ripened tomatoes,
   peeled, deseeded and
   chopped
4 spring onions, deseeded
   and finely chopped
3 tbsp mint leaves, finely
   chopped
4 tbsp coriander, finely
   chopped
¼ cucumber, peeled,
   deseeded and diced

1 Preheat the oven to 200°C/Gas 6. Place the red pepper (for the salad) on a baking tray and bake for 20 minutes. Transfer to a bowl, cover the bowl tightly with cling film and leave until cool enough to handle. Peel away the skin, then halve, deseed and chop finely. Set aside.

2 To make the charmoula, place all the ingredients in a food processor and blend to a paste.

3 For the salad, mix the tomato purée, wine vinegar and olive oil together in a large bowl and stir in the couscous along with some seasoning. Bring the stock to the boil and pour over the couscous. Cover with cling film and leave to

TO COOK THE FISH

olive oil, for brushing

salt and pepper

juice of ½ lemon, to taste

4–6 SERVINGS

stand for 15 minutes. Now fluff up the couscous with a fork, add the rest of the ingredients and toss to mix.

4　Check over the red mullet fillets for pin bones, while you heat up a griddle pan. Oil the fish fillets, then season with salt and pepper. Place the fillets, skin side down, on the griddle pan and cook for about 3 minutes. Carefully turn the fillets over, then drizzle over a little of the charmoula. Cook for a further 1 minute.

5　Pile the couscous salad on to warmed plates and top with the red mullet. Squeeze some lemon juice over the fish and drizzle plenty of charmoula around. Serve at once.

ROAST MONKFISH WITH RED WINE DRESSING

4 monkfish tails, about
   300g each
1 garlic clove, peeled and
   cut into slivers
handful of rosemary sprigs
salt and pepper
2 tbsp groundnut oil, for
   frying

RED WINE DRESSING
300ml red wine
2 tbsp red wine vinegar
2 tsp caster sugar
1 shallot, peeled and
   finely diced
1 tbsp oregano leaves,
   chopped
40ml olive oil

TO SERVE
rösti potatoes (see
   page 44)
oregano sprigs

4 SERVINGS

1 Skin the monkfish (unless already done) and remove the membrane by sliding a filleting knife between it and the flesh and working the membrane away. Try to remove all of it. Preheat the oven to 200°C/Gas 6.

2 Make 3 slits on each side of the monkfish fillets and insert a sliver of garlic and a rosemary sprig into each one. Season the fish with salt and pepper.

3 To make the red wine dressing, put the wine, wine vinegar and sugar into a pan, bring to the boil and let bubble to reduce to 4 tbsp. Pour into a bowl and add the shallot, oregano and some seasoning. Finally, whisk in the olive oil. Set aside; keep warm.

4 In the meantime, place a non-stick frying pan over a medium-high heat and add the groundnut oil. When almost smoking, add the monkfish fillets and fry until golden on both sides, about 4–5 minutes in total.

5 Transfer the fish to a baking tray and roast in the oven for 6 minutes. Remove from the oven, cover with foil and leave to rest for a few minutes. Pour the cooking juices into the red wine dressing and check the seasoning.

6 Place a rösti portion in the centre of each warmed plate. Lay the monkfish on top. Spoon some of the dressing over the fish and drizzle the rest around the plates. Garnish each serving with a sprig of oregano.

MACKEREL & SARDINES

There is never a shortage of mackerel – even I can catch them. They are available all year round, but I find they are at their best during April, May and June. Mackerel are attractive fish with patterned skin and silvery white bellies, which perhaps explains why *maquereau* (their French name) also means pimp! Their meaty, oily flesh has a very distinctive flavour and I absolutely love it.

The smell of sardines cooking on a barbecue reminds me so much of the Mediterranean. Like mackerel, sardines are rich, oily fish, but they are smaller with silvery blue skin and spiny scales along their bellies. Sardines may be bony and fiddly to prepare, but they are extremely tasty and well worth the effort.

The trouble with both mackerel and sardines is that they don't stay fresh for long, because their oils soon turn rancid, spoiling the flavour of the flesh. I would say they are definitely fish that you should catch, clean, gut, cook and eat on the same day, or the following day at the very latest.

Like sardines, mackerel are best grilled, seasoned with lots of black pepper and served with a tomato salad to cut the richness. Whole mackerel and sardines can also be barbecued or stuffed and baked (see page 138). Sardines are often 'butterflied' before cooking or rolling around a stuffing (see page 137).

Both sardines and mackerel are great matched with strong flavours – horseradish, mustard and lemon juice are all brilliant partners.

BAKED SARDINES WITH A HERBY STUFFING

Fresh sardines have a wonderful intense flavour and they are, of course, incredibly good for you. I like to cook them simply with herbs, lemon and breadcrumbs to cut the richness. All you need on the side is a fresh-tasting salad – such as rocket and fennel tossed in a light vinaigrette – and lots of crusty bread for a tasty lunch or light supper.

800g medium-small sardines, butterflied (see note)

olive oil, for cooking

50g white breadcrumbs (ideally a day old)

4 anchovy fillets in oil, drained

4 tbsp finely chopped parsley

1 tbsp finely chopped mint

1 small garlic clove, peeled and crushed

finely grated zest and juice of 1 lemon, or to taste

black pepper

4 SERVINGS

1   Preheat the oven to 200°C/Gas 6. Check over the prepared sardines for any bones and set aside on a board.

2   Heat a large non-stick frying pan and add a little oil. Add the breadcrumbs and fry, stirring frequently, until lightly golden. Tip on to a plate lined with kitchen paper to drain and cool, then transfer to a bowl.

3   Pat the anchovies dry, chop finely and mix into the breadcrumbs along with the parsley, mint, garlic, lemon zest and plenty of black pepper.

4   Lay the sardines, flesh side up, on a board and sprinkle with some of the breadcrumb mixture. Roll up from the head end, leaving the tail sticking up into the air. Place the rolled sardines in a gratin dish and sprinkle over the remaining breadcrumbs. Bake for 15–18 minutes, depending on size, until the sardines are cooked through and the breadcrumbs are golden.

5   Squeeze a little lemon juice over the sardines and serve with a rocket and fennel salad, and crusty bread.

NOTE   To butterfly a sardine, cut off the head, slit open the belly and remove the innards, then extend the cut down to the tail, but leave the tail intact. Lay the sardine, belly down, on a board and open out. Press firmly along the backbone with your thumbs to loosen it. Turn the fish over and pull out the backbone, then rinse and pat dry.

MACKEREL STUFFED WITH TAPENADE

4 good-sized mackerel,
    about 300g each,
    gutted and cleaned
    (heads removed)
1–2 tbsp sunflower oil
salt and pepper
flour, for dusting

TAPENADE

75g green olives, pitted
1 large garlic clove, peeled
4 salted anchovy fillets,
    rinsed and drained
25g capers, rinsed and
    drained
1 tbsp olive oil

**TOMATO AND BASIL
SALAD**

4 vine ripened tomatoes
1 tbsp good quality red
    wine vinegar
4 tbsp olive oil
1 red onion, peeled, halved
    and thinly sliced
small bunch of basil,
    leaves only, finely
    shredded

4 SERVINGS

1   Preheat the oven to 220°C/Gas 7. Extend the cut along the belly of each mackerel (used for gutting) from the head end right down to the tail. Lay the fish on a board and run a filleting knife either side of the backbone to loosen it from the flesh, cutting through the fine bones. Carefully pull the backbone away, leaving the tail on. Check the flesh for pin bones, removing them with tweezers.

2   To make the tapenade, put the olives, garlic, anchovies and capers on a board and chop them together finely until you have a coarse paste. Tip into a bowl and stir in the olive oil to combine. Stuff the mackerel with the paste and tie with kitchen string at intervals to secure.

3   Heat the sunflower oil in an ovenproof frying pan. Dust the mackerel with seasoned flour and fry on one side only until golden brown. Turn the fish and place the pan in the oven. Cook for about 6 minutes until the mackerel are ready.

4   In the meantime, prepare the salad. Slice the tomatoes into thin rounds. Whisk the wine vinegar and olive oil with a little salt and pepper to make a dressing.

5   To serve, arrange the tomatoes in the centre of serving plates. Top with the onion slices, scatter over some shredded basil and drizzle with the dressing. Snip the string and take off the fish, then gently place the mackerel on the tomatoes and scatter over some more basil. Serve immediately.

TURBOT, HALIBUT & SOLE

Turbot, along with sea bass, is my favourite fish. A large, flat fish with firm, flaky flesh, it tastes superb. The biggest ones have largely been fished out now, which is a real shame. Scarcity also accounts for their high price, but there is nothing like a good fresh turbot. To appreciate its fine flavour, I think it is best simply poached or grilled.

I've always been unlucky with halibut. It is not a fish caught by our local day boats and it seems to come into this country at least a week old and packed on ice. So, you get what you think is a nice fillet, but as you cut into it, the juices – along with the flavour – leak out, as they do from a frozen fish. However, you may be more fortunate. Really fresh halibut is a delicious meaty fish – great in curries.

Sole remains a popular fish in this country, especially the Dover sole – the most highly prized member of the family. At The New Angel, a plain grilled Dover sole with parsley butter and matchstick potatoes still flies out of the door. Freshness is of the utmost importance. Buy sole that are bright white on their underside and have coloured gills. The upper side varies a bit, but is usually greyish brown and mottled. Sole is usually sold gutted and skinned on the darker side or filleted. It is best cooked simply – poached, grilled or fried in butter.

The best way to buy all these flat fish is whole and fillet them yourself following the step-by-step guide overleaf. Bear in mind that a lot of weight is 'lost' in the trimmings, especially with smaller sole. Don't discard the trimmings though – the skeletons and heads are excellent for making stock (see page 247).

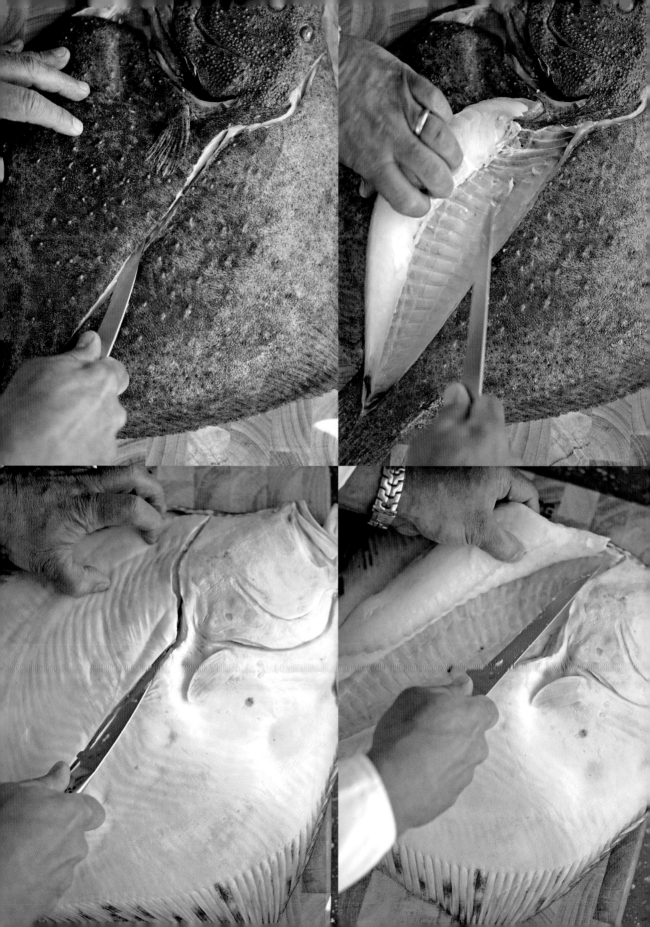

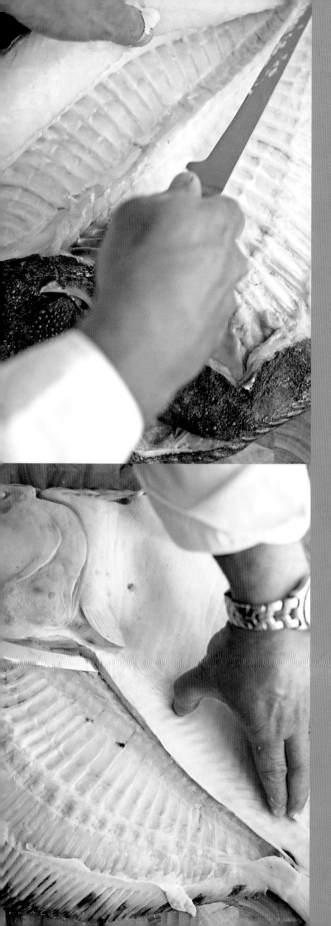

FILLETING A WHOLE FLAT FISH

Lay the flat fish (turbot, illustrated) on a board, dark side uppermost with the tail towards you. Using a filleting knife, cut down the centre of the fish along the backbone from head to tail.

From the head end, insert the knife again, this time at a slight angle, and carefully cut the fillet free, skimming the knife closely over the bones.

Return to the head end to detach the fillet from the ribs. If the fish has roe, poach in fish stock and serve separately. Turn the fish around and cut the second fillet on this side free in the same way. Now turn the fish over, white side up, and repeat the technique on the underside to free the other two fillets. You will have 4 fillets, two of them a bit smaller than the others, and a clean skeleton. Use the skeleton for making fish stock (see page 247).

To skin the fillets, if required, lay skin side down and cut 1cm flesh away at the tail end. With salted fingers, grasp the skin at this end, insert a knife between the skin and flesh and carefully cut the fillet free from the skin. Trim the fillets to neaten.

143

FILLET OF TURBOT BRAISED IN CIDER

I usually poach my favourite turbot in wine, but here I've used cider instead. It is important to buy a good quality dry cider, otherwise the sauce will become too sweet when you reduce it... besides this superior fish deserves fine partners.

4 turbot fillets, about
    160g each
2 medium courgettes,
    trimmed
1 small leek, trimmed and
    well washed
2 medium carrots, peeled
120g celeriac, peeled
120g potato, peeled
115g shallots, peeled
salt and pepper
60g unsalted butter
350ml dry cider
175ml fish stock (see
    page 247)
squeeze of lemon juice, to
    taste
50g baby spinach leaves

4 SERVINGS

1   Preheat the oven to 200°C/Gas 6. Skin the turbot fillets and trim to neaten, checking for any small bones.

2   Cut the courgettes, leek, carrots, celeriac, potato and shallots into 5mm dice, keeping them separate. Plunge the courgettes into a pan of boiling salted water, bring back to the boil, then immediately drain and refresh in iced water. Drain and keep aside. Repeat with the leek.

3   Repeat this blanching process with the carrots, celeriac and potato, but cook these vegetables until tender but still retaining a bite, before draining and refreshing.

4   Melt a knob of butter in a wide, shallow ovenproof pan, add the shallots and cook gently for a few minutes to soften slightly. Pour in the cider and bring to the boil.

5   Season the turbot fillets and lay them in the pan, then cover with buttered greaseproof paper and place in the oven. Cook for 4–8 minutes depending on the thickness of the fillets.

6   Meanwhile, bring half the stock to the boil in a pan and whisk in half of the remaining butter to emulsify. Add the blanched vegetables and warm through.

7   When the turbot fillets are cooked, transfer them to a plate and keep warm. Strain the juices into another pan, add the remaining stock and reduce by half over a high heat. Whisk in the rest of the butter. Check the seasoning and add lemon juice to taste.

8   Using a slotted spoon, arrange the diced vegetables in the centre of warmed serving plates. Return the pan to the heat, throw in the spinach and allow to wilt. Place the warmed turbot on top of the diced vegetables and spoon the wilted spinach alongside. Spoon over the sauce and serve at once.

LEMON SOLE CEVICHE

400g skinned lemon sole
  fillets
2 red chillies, deseeded
  and finely diced
juice of 4 limes
1 small chicory bulb,
  quartered lengthways
  and cut into 1cm strips
½ small red onion, peeled
  and finely sliced
2 tomatoes, skinned,
  deseeded and thinly
  sliced
1 green pepper, deseeded
  and thinly sliced
1 ripe avocado
3 tbsp chopped coriander
  leaves
100ml extra virgin olive oil
salt

6 SERVINGS

1   Cut the lemon sole fillets into 5mm strips and place in a shallow dish. Sprinkle with the diced chillies and pour over the lime juice. Toss to coat, then cover and leave in a cool place to marinate for 15 minutes. (The acid from the lime will cure the fish and turn it opaque.) If you prefer your fish 'cooked' a little more, leave it a bit longer.

2   Drain the fish of the lime juice and toss with the chicory, onion, tomatoes and green pepper. Halve, stone, peel and dice the avocado. Add to the fish mixture with the chopped coriander, pour over the olive oil and toss well. Leave to stand in a cool place for 10 minutes.

3   Season the ceviche well with salt and spoon into the centre of cool serving plates. Drizzle any remaining dressing around the plates. Serve immediately, as a starter.

POACHED HALIBUT WITH A SPINACH MAYONNAISE

If you are unable to obtain really fresh halibut, then use turbot fillets here instead. I like to serve this simple, elegant dish with new potatoes – cooked in their skins and tossed in butter – and green beans or a mixed salad.

4 halibut fillets, about
   170g each
salt and pepper
1.2 litres court bouillon
   (see page 247)

SPINACH AND HERB MAYONNAISE
20g baby spinach leaves
20 tarragon leaves
handful of flat parsley
   leaves
10 chives
10 mint leaves
1 small garlic clove, peeled
   and chopped
1 tsp Dijon mustard
2 egg yolks
300ml olive oil
juice of ½ lemon, or to
   taste

4 SERVINGS

1 Trim the halibut fillets and season with salt and pepper. Bring the court bouillon to the boil in a wide, shallow pan.

2 Meanwhile, for the mayonnaise, plunge the spinach and herb leaves into a large pan of boiling salted water for 10 seconds only. Drain and immerse in a bowl of cold water to stop further cooking. Squeeze the leaves dry and then chop finely.

3 Lay the halibut fillets in the court bouillon pan. Turn the heat down to just below a gentle simmer and put the lid on. Poach for 8–10 minutes until just cooked.

4 Meanwhile, make the mayonnaise. Put the garlic, mustard, egg yolks, chopped spinach and herb leaves into a food processor and whiz to combine, then with the motor running, slowly add the olive oil through the funnel. When all the oil is incorporated, season the mayonnaise with salt and pepper and add the lemon juice to taste.

5 By now, the halibut should be cooked. Lift out with a fish slice, drain well and place on warmed plates. Serve immediately with the herb mayonnaise.

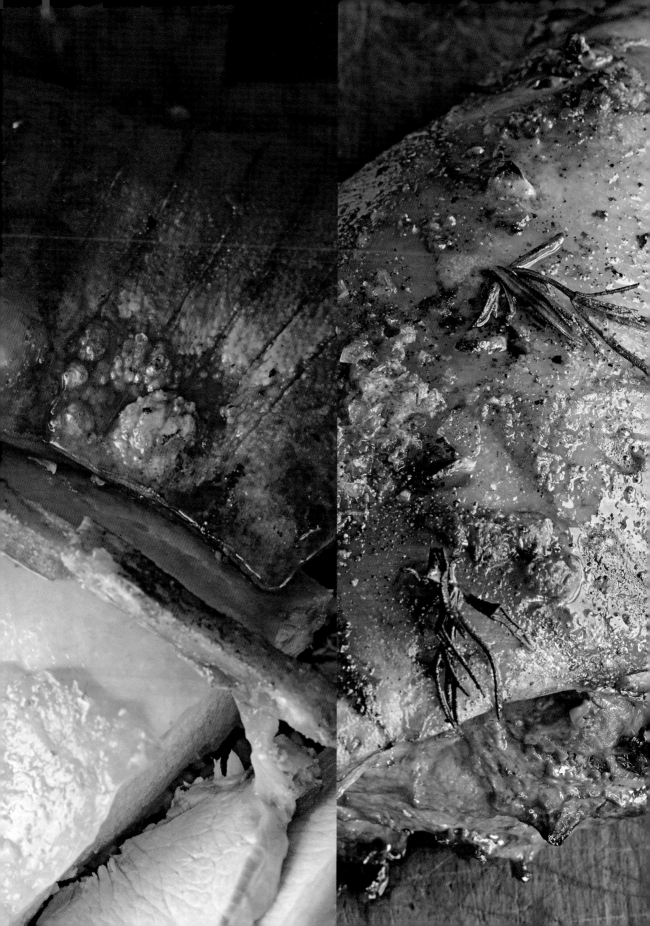

MEAT & POULTRY

BEEF

I am fortunate to know exactly where my beef comes from. Sourced locally from two farms in the South Hams, the cattle are slaughtered and hung locally, then delivered to my good friend and butcher, Bob Luscombe, in Totnes. He hangs them for a further 2 weeks, then delivers them direct to my restaurant. I consider these grass-fed animals to have the best possible flavour.

I cannot emphasise enough the importance of sourcing good quality beef. The quality is determined by the age of the animal, its breed, diet and whether it has been hung correctly. If you buy your meat from a good butcher, who knows his trade, you will appreciate the flavour of superior beef.

Mature beef is a deep, rich red colour and the cut surface should be shiny and slightly moist. Look for a good marbling of fat through the meat as this helps to keep it moist during cooking and improves the flavour. Cuts from the back half of the animal – sirloin, fillet, rump and topside – are the leanest and most expensive, but you can make great-tasting dishes from pretty much any part of the animal. Store all cuts, loosely wrapped, in the fridge and consume within a couple of days of buying.

I don't think you can beat a succulent roasted rib of beef with all the trimmings and fresh horseradish cream for a family Sunday lunch. Nice and easy homemade burgers always go down a treat with the kids, and the thought of a decent sirloin steak simply served with a spicy garlic butter and washed down with a glass of full-bodied red wine certainly makes my mouth water!

FILLET STEAKS WITH ANCHOIDE, CAPERS AND MUSTARD

I first ate this dish in the south of France. Anchovies seem to have a natural affinity with lamb, but I didn't believe they would work with beef. Trust me, they do... and it's a delicious combination. If you are able to source mature south Devon beef, so much the better.

4 beef fillet steaks, about
  150g each, or rump
  steaks, about 175g
salt and pepper
vegetable oil, for frying
60g capers, rinsed and
  dried
2 tbsp Dijon mustard

ANCHOIDE
300g anchovy fillets,
  drained
8 garlic cloves, peeled and
  chopped
100ml olive oil
3 tbsp chopped parsley
few tarragon sprigs,
  blanched briefly in
  boiling water
3 tbsp chives

4 SERVINGS

1   First make the anchoide. Put the anchovies in a food processor with the garlic, olive oil, parsley, tarragon and chives and purée until smooth. Add 50ml boiling water and whiz to a paste. Transfer to a screw-topped jar and keep in the fridge until required.

2   When ready to cook, preheat the oven to 200°C/Gas 6. Place an ovenproof skillet or heavy-based frying pan over a medium-high heat. Season each steak with a little salt. Add 1$\frac{1}{2}$ tbsp oil to the pan and when it is hot, add the steaks. Fry briefly to seal and brown on both sides.

3   Transfer the pan to the oven to finish cooking the steaks. Allow approximately 5 minutes for rare, or 7–8 minutes for medium, depending on thickness.

4   In the meantime, heat a 5cm depth of oil in a small, deep heavy-based pan. When hot, add the capers and deep-fry for 30 seconds until crispy. Drain on kitchen paper.

5   To serve, brush the top of each steak with a little Dijon mustard and place on warmed plates. Spoon over the anchovy sauce and scatter the crispy capers over the steaks and around the plate. Serve with a salad or warm fine beans and new potatoes.

ROASTED RIBEYE OF BEEF WITH A TOMATO AND HERB BEARNAISE

This is a great dish, so simple yet so full of flavour. I like to serve it with horseradish-flavoured mash and green beans or fresh peas when they are in season.

2 ribs of beef on the bone,
    about 1kg each
salt and pepper
20ml groundnut oil

TOMATO AND HERB BEARNAISE

1 quantity hollandaise
    sauce (see page 249)
30g tomato, skinned,
    deseeded and diced
1 tbsp chopped parsley
1 tbsp chopped or
    shredded basil
few tarragon sprigs,
    blanched (briefly in
    boiling water) and
    chopped

TO SERVE
2 bunches of watercress,
    trimmed and washed

4–6 SERVINGS

1   Preheat the oven to 180°C/Gas 4. Have the hollandaise sauce prepared and keep it warm (but not too hot or the sauce will split). Before you start to cook the beef, add the diced tomato to the hollandaise sauce, to give it a little time to infuse.

2   Place an ovenproof skillet or frying pan over a high heat to heat up. Season the ribs with salt and pepper. Add the oil to the hot pan and when it is almost smoking, put in the seasoned ribs. Cook for about 2 minutes on each side to colour as much as possible. This will give the beef a beautiful, caramelised flavour.

3   Transfer the pan to the oven to finish cooking. Allow about 8–10 minutes for rare or 12–14 minutes for medium, depending on how well cooked you like your beef. Remove from the oven and leave to rest in a warm place for about 5 minutes.

4   While the meat is resting, stir the herbs through the hollandaise and check the seasoning. Carve the ribs on a wooden board. Arrange the meat on warmed plates and garnish with the watercress. Hand the sauce around separately in a sauceboat.

CALVES LIVER WITH ORANGE AND CARROTS

A delicious way to enjoy tender calves liver. Meat glaze adds a real depth of flavour to the sauce, so I hope you have some to hand in the freezer! Spinach is an ideal accompaniment.

2 oranges

4 garlic cloves, peeled

90g butter

6 shallots, peeled and
chopped

1 large onion, peeled and
chopped

30ml sherry vinegar

30g sugar, plus 1 tsp

1 litre chicken stock
(see page 247)

1 thyme sprig

1 bay leaf

3 large carrots, peeled

salt and pepper

30ml white wine vinegar

1 tarragon sprig

60ml meat glaze
(see page 248), optional

6 slices of calves liver,
about 120g each, skin
removed

60g clarified butter
(see page 251)

6 SERVINGS

1   Using a swivel peeler, finely pare the zest from 1 orange (avoid the pith) and cut into fine strips. Squeeze the juice from both oranges, strain and set aside. Chop 3 garlic cloves.

2   Melt half the butter in a heavy-based saucepan, add the chopped garlic, shallots and onion and cook gently to soften but not colour. Add the orange zest strips and sherry vinegar and reduce until dry. Sprinkle in the 30g sugar and cook over a low heat for 10 minutes or until the onions are caramelised. Pour in the orange juice, then the stock, bring to the boil and skim. Add the thyme and bay leaf, lower the heat and simmer for 20 minutes.

3   Meanwhile, cut the carrots into batons and cook in salted water until just tender. Leave to cool naturally.

4   Heat the wine vinegar and 1 tsp sugar in a small pan, then boil to reduce to a caramel. Before it gets too dark, add 2 tbsp water, the remaining garlic and the tarragon. Boil and reduce, whisking in 15g butter. When syrupy, take off the heat, remove the garlic and season with salt and pepper.

5   Whiz the orangey sauce in a blender until smooth. Strain through a fine sieve into a clean pan. Bring to the boil, skim and reduce by half, then add the meat glaze, if using. Whisk in the remaining butter in pieces and season to taste.

6   When ready to serve, season the liver. Place a large heavy-based frying pan over a high heat. Add the clarified butter and heat until smoking. Lay the liver slices in the pan and cook on a high heat for 30 seconds until beads of blood show on the surface. Turn and cook for another 30 seconds.

7   At the same time, heat up the tarragon glaze, add the carrot batons and toss to glaze and heat through.

8   Remove the liver from the pan as soon as it's ready. Lay on warmed plates and surround with the carrots. Spoon over some of the orange sauce, handing the rest separately.

OXTAIL AND HERB DUMPLINGS BRAISED IN ALE

A hearty English dish, best eaten when it's freezing cold and you're starving hungry. Trust me, it is very filling... and very comforting.

olive oil, for frying

3 large onions, peeled and sliced

1 medium oxtail, cut into pieces

flour, for dusting

salt and pepper

450ml brown ale

400ml chicken stock (see page 247)

1 tbsp light brown sugar

HERB DUMPLINGS

75g self-raising flour

35g shredded suet

1 tbsp chopped thyme leaves

TO GARNISH

chopped parsley

4 SERVINGS

1   Preheat the oven to 170°C/Gas 3. Heat a little olive oil in a large heavy-based frying pan over a medium heat and, when it is almost smoking, add the onions. Cook, stirring occasionally until soft and golden brown. Remove from the pan and place in a casserole dish.

2   Roll the oxtail pieces in the flour to coat and season well with salt and pepper. Heat a little more oil in the frying pan and again when it is nearly starting to smoke add the oxtail pieces. Fry, turning, until well coloured on all sides, then add to the onions in the casserole.

3   Pour the ale into the frying pan while still on the heat and scrape up the sediment from the bottom of the pan with a wooden spoon. Now add the stock and sugar. Simmer for 2 minutes, then pour over the oxtail and onions. Place a lid on the casserole and cook in the oven for 3 hours.

4   In the meantime, make the dumplings. Sift the flour into a bowl and mix in the suet, chopped thyme leaves and some salt and pepper. Mix in just enough water to form a dough that comes away from the sides of the bowl. Divide into 4 equal pieces and shape into balls.

5   About 25 minutes before the end of the cooking time, add the dumplings to the casserole and return to the oven. When ready, the oxtail should be meltingly tender and the dumplings cooked through.

6   Serve in warmed bowls, sprinkled with chopped parsley and accompanied by glazed carrots and peas or fine beans.

LAMB

This is finer grained and naturally more tender than other meats, such as beef or game, and I love it. The best lamb comes in the early spring, and I always make the most of it. When you cook lamb in season, you will discern a real difference.

The fat on the first new season's lamb is very sweet, almost white and crumbly, and the meat will be fairly pale in colour. Expect all joints to be smaller than average, because they are less developed. If a lamb is allowed to go on too long, it is no longer lamb but mutton. Cheaper cuts and older animals are great for braising and pot roasts. Inexpensive cuts like lamb shanks work well in the winter months if you cook them slowly and serve them with a robust, rich sauce. Shoulder of lamb is a flavourful joint for roasting, though it is fattier and harder to carve on the bone than leg.

Of the prime cuts, loin is easy to cook and makes a sweet juicy roast. A whole leg of new season's lamb is beautiful roasted, and you can treat a knuckle end from a larger animal in the same way later in the year. Leg steaks and chump chops (cut from the loin) are delicious grilled or barbecued and served with a piquant herb and anchovy butter (page 249).

Lamb's kidneys, sweetbreads and liver from new season's lamb are, in my opinion, as good as any offal from veal. One dish I am looking to add to the New Angel menu is stuffed lamb's trotters, which are as delicious and succulent as you would get off a young pig.

Because lamb is so delicate, you must take care to avoid overcooking it. Whether grilled, fried or roasted, it should be pink and juicy inside.

ROASTED LEG OF LAMB WITH MINTED CRUSHED PEAS

The first crop of peas are small and deliciously sweet – the perfect match for a succulent, sweet leg of new season's lamb. If young, fresh peas are not available, however, you can use frozen ones.

1 leg of new season's
    lamb, about 1.75kg–2kg
8 salted anchovy fillets,
    halved
3 garlic cloves, peeled and
    cut into slivers
15 rosemary sprigs
a little olive oil
salt and pepper
900g potatoes (preferably
    Maris Piper)
250g freshly shelled peas
    (or frozen ones,
    defrosted)
15g butter
handful of mint leaves,
    chopped

4–6 SERVINGS

1   Preheat the oven to 220°C/Gas 7. Using a small, sharp knife, make lots of small incisions all over the leg. Now insert small pieces of anchovy, garlic and rosemary into the slits. Rub the leg with the olive oil and season well with salt and pepper.

2   Place in a roasting tray in the middle of the oven and roast for approximately 20 minutes per 500g, plus an extra 20 minutes, basting frequently.

3   Meanwhile, peel the potatoes and quarter or cut into large pieces. Add to a large pan of salted water, bring to the boil and par-boil for 5 minutes, while you heat up a shallow roasting tin in the oven. Drain the potatoes and let the excess moisture steam off. Add a splash of oil to the hot roasting tin, then tip in the potatoes, drizzle with olive oil and season well. Roast in the oven on a shelf above the lamb, turning once or twice during cooking. The potatoes are ready when they are golden brown and crispy all over.

4   Meanwhile, prepare the crushed peas. If using fresh peas, cook them in boiling salted water for about 5 minutes until tender; drain well. Tip the blanched (or the defrosted frozen) peas into a food processor and pulse briefly to a coarse texture, making sure you don't go too far and end up with a purée.

5   When the lamb is ready, transfer to a warmed platter, cover loosely with foil and leave to rest for 10–15 minutes before carving. Meanwhile, transfer the peas to a saucepan and warm through with the butter and some seasoning. Stir in the chopped mint.

6   Carve the lamb and serve with the roast potatoes and crushed peas.

PREPARING BEST END OF LAMB

Score through the fat crossways, about a third of the way down the rack through to the bone. Using a very sharp knife, carefully cut away the fat from the upper part of the rack by working the knife along between the bones and fat to remove it in one piece. Then trim away the skin from the lower part of the rack, to leave a thin, even layer of fat covering the meat (this helps to keep the lamb moist during cooking). Now work the knife between the individual bones, trimming away the fat neatly. Finally, take a sharp meat cleaver and chop off the tips of the bones for a neat finish.

BEST END OF LAMB WITH CARAMELISED ORANGE AND HAZELNUT SALAD

Early new season's lamb is wonderfully delicate and the fat is deliciously sweet. The last thing it needs is a sauce to mask the subtle flavours. Here I've served it with a simple salad dressed with a hazelnut vinaigrette and a little orange to cut the richness. Dauphinoise potatoes (see page 47) are the perfect accompaniment.

3 French-trimmed best
   ends of lamb (each with
   6 bones)
salt and pepper
1 tbsp vegetable oil, plus
   extra to oil
2 oranges
40g caster sugar
2 tbsp clarified butter
   (see page 251)
6 generous handfuls of
   mixed salad leaves
   (such as wild rocket,
   red chard, baby spinach)
handful of hazelnuts,
   lightly toasted
90ml hazelnut vinaigrette
   (see page 250)

6 SERVINGS

1   Preheat the oven to 200°C/Gas 6. Season the best ends with salt and pepper. Heat the oil in a large roasting pan on the hob. One at a time, sear the racks in the hot oil, turning them until golden brown all over.

2   Return all 3 lamb racks to the pan and roast in the oven for 10–15 minutes, according to how rare you like your lamb, turning once.

3   Meanwhile, preheat the grill. Peel and segment the oranges, removing all pith and membrane, then pat dry. Lay the segments on an oiled tray. Mix the sugar with the clarified butter and spoon over the oranges. Place under the hot grill for a few minutes to caramelise.

4   Remove the lamb from the oven and leave to rest in a warm place for 10–15 minutes while you prepare the salad.

5   Toss the mixed salad leaves with the toasted hazelnuts and vinaigrette. Place on one side of each serving plate.

6   Carve down between the lamb bones to divide the best ends into cutlets. Arrange 3 cutlets on each plate and place the warm caramelised orange segments alongside. Serve with dauphinoise potatoes, or new potatoes if you prefer.

GRILLED LAMB LEG STEAKS WITH A SPICY MARINADE

These steaks are great for barbecues. For optimum flavour, you need to marinate the lamb well in advance – ideally overnight. Use young lamb and get your butcher to bone out the meat and prepare the steaks for you if possible.

1kg boned leg of lamb, cut into 8 steaks

MARINADE

400ml olive oil

3 tbsp Worcestershire sauce

1 tbsp Tabasco sauce

2 anchovy fillets, finely chopped

1 rosemary sprig, leaves only, finely chopped

2 thyme sprigs, leaves only, finely chopped

1 bay leaf

1 garlic clove, peeled and finely chopped

salt and pepper

pinch of sugar

juice of 1 lemon

8 SERVINGS

1 Place the lamb steaks in a large shallow dish. Put all the ingredients for the marinade in a bowl and whisk together. Pour the marinade over the lamb and leave to marinate for at least 5–6 hours (preferably overnight) to allow the flavours to penetrate the meat.

2 Preheat the grill to high or light the barbecue and wait until the flames die right down so you are just left with the ambers glowing red.

3 Remove the lamb steaks from the dish, reserving the marinade. Grill or barbecue for 4–5 minutes each side, basting them occasionally with the marinade. Do so sparingly if barbecuing, otherwise the oil will cause the coals to flame.

4 Serve the lamb steaks with roasted vegetables or a salad. Yoghurt flavoured with freshly chopped mint and lightly seasoned is a delicious accompaniment.

DEVILLED NEW SEASON LAMB'S KIDNEYS

Only use young lamb's kidneys, as these are really tender and sweet in flavour. Kidneys from older animals are too strong for my taste. The piquant flavours of the marinade cut the richness of the kidneys to delicious effect. Use veal kidneys instead if you prefer.

8 new season lamb's
   kidneys

MARINADE

1 tbsp English mustard

1 tbsp Meaux mustard

3 tbsp olive oil

2 egg yolks

pinch of salt

pinch of cayenne pepper

1 tsp anchovy paste

1 tsp Worcestershire sauce

TO SERVE

4 slices white bread

1 tbsp finely chopped flat
   leaf parsley

4 SERVINGS

1   Peel the outer membrane off the kidneys, then halve them horizontally and snip out the white cores with kitchen scissors. Set aside.

2   Next, put all the ingredients for the marinade into a medium bowl and whisk well to combine. Add the kidneys, turn to coat well, then cover the bowl and leave to marinate in a cool place for 2–3 hours.

3   When ready to serve, preheat the grill to high. Place the kidneys on a sturdy baking tray, spoon over the marinade and cook under the grill for 2–3 minutes. Turn the kidneys over, baste well with the marinade and grill for a further 2–3 minutes or until cooked to your liking.

4   In the meantime, toast the bread in your toaster. Place a slice of toast on each warmed plate and place the kidneys on top. Spoon the cooking juices over and sprinkle with the chopped parsley. Serve at once.

PORK & HAM

There are many different cuts of pork and its cured forms – bacon and ham. In fact you can make a meal out of literally every part of a pig, even the testicles, although perhaps understandably these aren't as popular nowadays!

Sadly, not all pork is as tasty as it should be, because most pigs today are raised indoors on a restricted diet. I buy pigs that originate from low-density farms with open sties – their meat tastes far superior. I strongly recommend you buy pork from a good butcher, with a high turnover so its freshness can be guaranteed.

When you are choosing a joint for roasting, look for a good covering of fat – 1cm on a loin of pork is a good thickness. Don't buy deep red coloured pork, as this indicates the meat is from an older animal. Similarly, avoid meat that looks wet and slippery or that has waxy-looking fat, as it won't be of good quality. Instead pick cuts with firm pink flesh and white fat. Store in the fridge for no longer than 2 days before consuming. If you are buying a traditionally cured ham joint, you will need to soak it before cooking, for up to 24 hours.

One of my favourite simple meals is based on pork. I buy a pork belly, cut it into 5cm chunks and throw it into a pot with diced leek, chopped garlic and thyme sprigs, then cover with white wine and cook gently until it's beautifully caramelised and golden brown, and the wine has evaporated. Eaten hot with mash and green beans, it is divine, though sometimes I pick out the caramelised pork pieces, let them go cold, then serve with French bread, a bowl of gherkins and a glass of Sancerre or Vouvray Sec. Try it!

GUINNESS GLAZED HAM WITH BROAD BEANS AND PARSLEY SAUCE

1.5kg boneless gammon
   joint
1 onion, peeled and
   halved
1 carrot, peeled and
   roughly chopped
1 celery stick, roughly
   chopped
1 leek, washed and
   roughly chopped
1kg broad beans, freshly
   podded
30 cloves
4 tsp English mustard
4 tsp demerara sugar
500ml Guinness
knob of butter

PARSLEY SAUCE

70g unsalted butter
45g plain flour
250ml milk
20g finely chopped
   parsley
salt and pepper
3 tbsp single cream

8–10 SERVINGS

1   Unless the gammon has been pre-soaked, you'll need to soak it in cold water overnight to draw out excess salt.

2   The next day, drain the gammon and place in a large saucepan with the onion, carrot, celery and leek. Cover with water, bring to the boil and skim, then lower the heat and simmer gently for about 1½ hours. Using a large fork, lift the gammon out of the pan on to a board and leave to cool for at least 15–20 minutes. Strain the liquor and reserve.

3   In the meantime, blanch the broad beans in boiling water for 3 minutes, then drain, refresh under cold water and slip the beans out of their tough outer skins; set aside.

4   Preheat the oven to 200°C/Gas 6. Remove the skin from the gammon leaving as much of the fat on the meat as possible. Score the fat in a diamond pattern, stud with the cloves and brush the mustard evenly over the gammon. Sprinkle with the sugar and press it on firmly.

5   Place the ham in a roasting tray, pour over the Guinness and add a small ladleful of the reserved ham stock. Bake in the oven, basting frequently, for 30–40 minutes or until the ham is glazed and the liquor has reduced to a sticky syrup.

6   Meanwhile, make the parsley sauce. Melt the butter in a pan, add the flour and cook, stirring for 1 minute. Then gradually add the milk, followed by 300ml of the ham stock, whisking continuously to keep the sauce smooth. Cook, stirring, for 2–3 minutes, then pass the sauce through a fine sieve into a clean pan. Add the chopped parsley and season to taste (you may only need pepper, as the ham stock will probably provide enough salt). Set aside until needed.

7   When cooked, rest the ham for 5 minutes before carving. To serve, warm the broad beans in a pan with a knob of butter and seasoning. Reheat the parsley sauce and stir in the cream. Lift the glazed gammon on to a board and carve into slices. Serve with the broad beans and parsley sauce.

ROAST LOIN OF PORK WITH A CIDER SAUCE

You can use leg or shoulder of pork for this recipe, though loin is my first choice here. It carves beautifully. You simply remove the crisp cracking in one piece, then carve the pork into slices and serve each portion with a generous piece of crackling.

2kg loin of pork

salt and pepper

1–2 tbsp groundnut oil

CIDER SAUCE

20ml groundnut oil

500g pork bones (ask your butcher), chopped small

1 large onion, peeled and chopped

1 large carrot, peeled and chopped

1 celery stick, chopped

2 garlic cloves, peeled and crushed

1 bay leaf

2 thyme sprigs

1 Granny Smith apple, chopped

300ml dry cider

400ml chicken stock (see page 247)

TO SERVE

baked apples with walnuts and prunes (see page 201)

glazed potatoes cooked in cider (see page 44)

6 SERVINGS

1   Preheat the oven to 200°C/Gas 6. Season the pork loin generously with salt, rubbing it in well to encourage a crispy crackling, then season with pepper. Place a roasting tray or large ovenproof pan over a high heat, add the groundnut oil and heat almost to smoking point. Add the pork loin and turn to seal all over. Transfer to the oven and roast for 1½ hours or until cooked through.

2   In the meantime, prepare the cider sauce. Place a heavy-based pan over a medium-high heat and heat up, then add the oil. When it is almost smoking, add the pork bones and cook, stirring frequently, until they are deep golden in colour.

3   Add the vegetables, garlic and herbs, lower the heat and cook for 8–10 minutes or until softened and golden. Add the chopped apple and cider. Bring to the boil and simmer to reduce by half, then add the stock. Bring back to the boil, skim and simmer again for 20–25 minutes.

4   Pass the sauce through a fine sieve into a clean pan and simmer to reduce by at least half, to thicken and concentrate the flavour; keep warm. Have the baked apples and potatoes ready and hot.

5   Remove the pork from the oven, transfer to a warmed platter and rest in a warm place for 10 minutes. Pour off the fat from the roasting pan, then add the meat juices to the sauce. Carve the pork, first removing the crackling in one piece to make it easier to do so.

6   Arrange the pork slices on warmed serving plates. Add a portion of crackling, a baked stuffed apple and a potato or two to each plate. Serve immediately, accompanied by the cider sauce in a sauceboat. Braised red cabbage goes well with this dish.

HONEY GLAZED PORK SHOULDER WITH PICKLED VEGETABLES

This is a great sweet and sour alternative to the usual roast pork. It is also good cold with a salad. The pickled vegetables can be prepared ahead and kept in the fridge for up to 3 days.

1.5kg pork shoulder joint

salt and pepper

4 large onions, peeled and thinly sliced

100ml olive oil

PICKLED VEGETABLES

100g baby carrots, peeled

100g baby turnips, peeled

100g baby fennel, trimmed

100g baby beetroot, peeled

100g baby onions, peeled

300ml white wine vinegar

100g soft brown sugar

100g caster sugar

1 thyme sprig

1 bay leaf

6 black peppercorns

10 coriander seeds, crushed

1 garlic clove, peeled and sliced

SPICED HONEY GLAZE

6 tbsp clear honey

10g Chinese five spice

8 cloves

10 coriander seeds

1 star anise

2 garlic cloves, peeled and crushed

4 SERVINGS

1 Preheat the oven to 180°C/Gas 4. Score the pork skin with a sharp knife and season with salt and pepper, rubbing the salt in well, as this will help crisp the skin.

2 Scatter the sliced onions in a deep roasting tray and place the pork on top. Pour over the olive oil and roast in the oven for about 1½ hours.

3 Now prepare the pickled vegetables (or do this ahead). Blanch the vegetables separately until barely tender – they need to retain a slight crunch. Refresh in iced water, drain and reserve. Put the wine vinegar, sugars and 100ml water in a saucepan and dissolve over a low heat, then add the herbs, spices and garlic. Bring to the boil, lower heat and simmer for 5–8 minutes. Take off the heat, add the vegetables and leave to cool.

4 Baste the pork with the juices and if the onions seem dry, add a little water to the tray. Roast in the oven for a further 1 hour. Meanwhile, warm the honey with 6 tbsp water until smooth, then take off the heat. Crush the spices and add to the honey with the garlic.

5 Remove the pork shoulder from the oven and turn the setting to 200°C/Gas 6. Discard any blackened onions from the edges, then pour the honey mix over the pork. Return to the oven and cook for a further 20–30 minutes or until the pork is glazed a deep golden brown colour.

6 Transfer the pork to a warmed platter, cover loosely with foil and rest for 10–15 minutes. Spoon the pickled vegetables on to warmed serving plates. Slice the pork and arrange alongside. Place the roasting tray over a medium heat, add a little water and stir to deglaze and combine with the juices. Strain this liquor over the pork and serve.

SPICED AND BRAISED PORK BELLY WITH GLAZED BEETROOT

This is a delicious way to cook pork belly. The cider and beetroot syrup and the apple and tarragon compote cut the richness perfectly. Get your butcher to skin and de-bone the pork belly for you if possible.

1.5kg piece pork belly,
   boned and skinned
salt and pepper
20g mixed spices (allspice,
   coriander seeds, cloves,
   cinnamon, juniper)
100g unsalted butter
50ml olive oil
1 large carrot, peeled and
   chopped
1 large onion, peeled and
   chopped
2 celery sticks, trimmed
   and chopped
2 garlic cloves, peeled and
   crushed
2 thyme sprigs
1 bay leaf
1 Granny Smith apple,
   cored and chopped
2 litres chicken stock
   (see page 247)

TO SERVE

apple and tarragon
   compote (see page 201)
glazed beetroot in cider
   vinegar (see page 38)

4 SERVINGS

1   Preheat the oven to 180°C/Gas 4. Lay the pork, skinned side down, on a board and season with salt and pepper. Crush the spices to a powder, using a food processor or pestle and mortar and rub over the pork flesh. Roll up the pork and secure tightly with string.

2   Heat the butter and olive oil in a deep roasting tray or flameproof casserole until the butter has melted and it is almost smoking. Add the pork belly and turn to colour evenly on all sides until golden brown. Remove the pork and set aside.

3   Add the vegetables to the roasting tray and cook over a medium heat until softened and golden brown. Add the garlic, herbs and apple.

4   Return the pork to the tray and pour on the stock. Cover with foil and cook in the oven for 1 hour. Remove the foil and cook for a further 1–1½ hours until soft to the touch, basting frequently and turning the pork occasionally.

5   Leave to cool for at least 1 hour, then remove the pork from the liquor and set aside. Pass the liquor through a fine sieve into a pan, bring to the boil and reduce by one-third. Check the seasoning.

6   When ready to serve, preheat the oven to 180°C/Gas 4. Cut the pork belly into four equal portions, removing the string. Place in a casserole, cover with the reduced liquor and gently heat through in the oven, basting frequently to give a beautiful, glossy and sticky glaze.

7   Arrange the pork belly on warmed plates with the apple and tarragon compote and the glazed beetroot. Spoon some of the glaze over the meat and around the plate. Serve at once, with dauphinoise potatoes (see page 47) if you like.

GAME

It's great when game comes into season during the autumn months. A whole door in the culinary world opens and I love to take advantage of this different produce and cook it as a tasty alternative to other meats.

From September, rabbit is very popular in the restaurant – probably because it is similar, although stronger in flavour, to chicken. Rabbit goes well with strong flavours including garlic, mustard and herbs. I especially like it with prunes. Venison is similar in texture to lamb, though it is a lot leaner. Cranberries are a good partner for this meat. The best time to buy pheasant is from October through to the end of January. The flesh has a subtle gamey flavour and is very lean and firm. Pheasant lends itself well to spices. Similarly spices, such as cinnamon and nutmeg, work well with pigeon as they bring out the natural sweetness of the flesh. A red or white wine sauce will also complement game well.

I often serve garlic and parsley croûtes with game for a crisp contrast. To make these, cut a baguette into thin slices, sprinkle with olive oil and bake at 200°C/Gas 6 for about 5 minutes until golden. Rub with a cut garlic clove and dip one edge into chopped parsley to coat.

Game chips are another traditional accompaniment that I like to serve. To make these, peel 2 medium potatoes and slice on a mandolin or with a sharp knife, into wafer-thin discs. Wash to remove excess starch, then drain and dry thoroughly on kitchen paper. Deep-fry the potato slices in hot oil at 190°C until crisp and brown, drain on kitchen paper and season with salt to serve.

ROAST LOIN OF VENISON WITH A GREEN PEPPERCORN SAUCE

Ask your butcher for the bones, left from boning out the venison loin to make a full-flavoured stock for the sauce.

600g boned loin of
  venison, plus bones
4 tbsp sunflower oil
500g venison bones,
  chopped small
1 onion, peeled and
  chopped
2 tbsp red wine vinegar
500ml red wine
500ml chicken stock (see
  page 247)
1 thyme sprig
1 bay leaf
6 juniper berries, crushed
1 garlic clove, peeled and
  crushed
salt and pepper
10g green peppercorns,
  crushed
25ml double cream

TO SERVE

glazed beetroot in cider
  vinegar (see page 38)
game chips (see page 176)

4 SERVINGS

1   Trim the venison and set aside. Place a large saucepan over a high heat. Add 2 tbsp oil and, when almost smoking, add the venison bones. Fry, stirring often, until browned. Add the onion and cook until browned. Pour off any excess oil into a bowl. Add the wine vinegar, bring to the boil and reduce to a sticky syrup that coats the bones.

2   Pour in the red wine, bring back to the boil and cook for about 3 minutes, then add the stock. Return to the boil and add the thyme, bay leaf, juniper berries and garlic. Skim, then lower the heat to a simmer and cook for 1 hour. Strain through a fine sieve into a clean pan and boil to reduce by two-thirds. You will need about 200ml.

3   Preheat the oven to 200°C/Gas 6. Season the venison with salt and pepper. Place a roasting pan on the hob over a medium-high heat. Pour in the remaining 2 tbsp oil and, as soon as it starts to smoke, add the loin of venison and brown all over. Transfer to the oven to finish cooking. Allow about 7 minutes for rare, 10 minutes for medium.

4   Meanwhile, pour the reduced sauce through a muslin-lined sieve into another pan and bring to a simmer. Season with salt and the crushed green peppercorns, then stir in the cream. Check the seasoning and keep warm, but don't let the sauce boil or it may split.

5   When the venison is cooked to your liking, transfer to a warmed plate and leave to rest in a warm place for about 5 minutes. Cut the loin into four equal pieces. Spoon a pool of sauce on to each warmed plate and top with the venison. Add the beetroot and game chips and serve, with green beans or Savoy cabbage.

RABBIT AND PRUNE CASSEROLE

Get your butcher to joint the rabbits and remember you will need to put them to marinate the evening before. Accompany with mashed potatoes, green beans or stir-fried cabbage and a glass of full-bodied red wine.

2 wild rabbits, jointed

75cl bottle red wine

2 thyme sprigs

1 bay leaf

4 juniper berries, crushed

2 flat leaf parsley sprigs

1 tsp black peppercorns,
   crushed

250g unsmoked bacon

salt and pepper

3 tbsp olive oil

50g unsalted butter

2 onions, peeled and diced

75ml red wine vinegar

1 tbsp redcurrant jelly

24 pitted prunes

50g raisins

750ml chicken stock
   (see page 247)

TO SERVE

garlic and parsley croûtes
   (see page 176)

4 SERVINGS

1   The evening before, put the rabbit joints into a large bowl. Pour the wine over them and add the thyme, bay leaf, juniper berries, parsley and peppercorns. Cover with cling film and refrigerate overnight.

2   The next day, cut the bacon into lardons, 5mm wide, put into a pan of cold water and bring to the boil. Drain and pat dry. Pan-fry, without extra fat, until crisp and golden. Drain on kitchen paper and reserve.

3   Drain the rabbit in a colander over another bowl to save the liquor. Put the rabbit on a board and season with salt. Place a large frying pan over a medium-high heat to heat up, then add the olive oil and 20g of the butter. When hot, fry the rabbit joints, in batches, until browned all over, then transfer to a flameproof casserole dish.

4   Preheat the oven to 200°C/Gas 6. Strain the red wine marinade through a fine sieve into another saucepan and bring to the boil. Skim, then boil to reduce by half.

5   Meanwhile, melt the remaining butter in the frying pan and cook the onions until softened. Add the wine vinegar and redcurrant jelly and cook until syrupy, then spoon over the rabbit. Add the reserved bacon, prunes and raisins.

6   Pour the reduced marinade over the rabbit and add the stock. Bring to a simmer on the hob, then cover and cook in the oven for about 45 minutes until the rabbit is tender.

7   When ready, lift out the rabbit, prunes, raisins and bacon with a slotted spoon and put them in a deep serving dish; keep warm. Place the casserole over a high heat and boil the sauce to reduce by about one-third. Season with pepper and add a little more salt if needed. Strain the sauce through a fine sieve over the rabbit and serve immediately, with the garlic and parsley croûtes.

PIGEON BREASTS WITH A BEARNAISE SAUCE

12 wild pigeon breasts

salt and pepper

4 garlic cloves, peeled and
   halved

200ml whipping cream

18 baby carrots

18 baby turnips

300ml vegetable stock
   (see page 248)

knob of butter

BEARNAISE SAUCE

150g butter

3 large shallots, peeled
   and finely chopped

2 garlic cloves, peeled and
   halved

6 white peppercorns,
   crushed

25ml white wine vinegar

50ml double cream

2 egg yolks

125g hot clarified butter
   (see page 251)

lemon juice, to taste

pinch of cayenne pepper,
   to taste

1 tsp each finely chopped
   chervil, chives, parsley

1/2 tsp finely chopped
   tarragon

TO SERVE

game chips (see page 176)

6 SERVINGS

1   Season the pigeon breasts with salt and pepper, place in a shallow dish and scatter over the garlic. Pour over the cream, then cover with cling film and set aside.

2   Wash and peel the carrots and turnips, retaining their leafy tops. Cook separately in boiling salted water until just tender. Drain and allow to cool naturally.

3   To make the sauce, melt 60g butter in a pan and add the shallots, garlic, crushed peppercorns and wine vinegar. Reduce until dry, then whisk in 1 tbsp hot water and the cream; keep warm. Melt the remaining butter gently in another pan, season and keep warm.

4   Put the egg yolks and 1 tbsp water in a heatproof bowl over a pan of simmering water and whisk vigorously over a low heat until thick enough to form a ribbon when the whisk is lifted. Take the bowl off the heat and whisk in the hot clarified butter, adding lemon juice, salt and cayenne pepper to taste. Pour into a warm pan and add the shallot and butter mix. Stir in the chopped herbs and check the seasoning.

5   When ready to serve, preheat the grill to high. Cook the pigeon breasts under the grill for 3 minutes on each side. Meanwhile, reheat the carrots and turnips in the stock with a knob of butter, then drain.

6   To assemble, spoon a pool of béarnaise sauce into the middle of each plate. Halve the pigeon breasts and place on the sauce, piling them one on top of the other. Place the carrots and turnips alongside, with a stack of game chips on the other side of the plate. Serve immediately, with the rest of the sauce in a sauceboat.

PHEASANT TERRINE

1 oven-ready hen
   pheasant
8 tbsp oil
1 carrot, peeled and sliced
1 onion, peeled and diced
salt and white pepper
2 garlic cloves, peeled
20 juniper berries
8 white peppercorns
100g lean pork
250g pork fat
grated zest of 1 orange
grated zest of 1 lemon
15g butter
2 shallots, peeled and
   diced
1½ tbsp brandy
65g shelled pistachio nuts,
   skinned and chopped
250g thin pork fat slices
   (lardo)

8 SERVINGS

1   Cut the legs and breasts from the pheasant, trim and set aside. Chop the carcass. Heat 5 tbsp oil in a heavy-based frying pan over a medium-high heat, add the bones and trimmings and fry until well coloured. Add the vegetables, 2 litres water, 1 tsp salt, 1 garlic clove, 8 juniper berries and the peppercorns. Bring to the boil and simmer for 1 hour. Strain into a clean pan and boil to reduce to 250ml.

2   Cut the meat from the pheasant legs and put in a bowl with the pork and pork fat. Crush 8 juniper berries and the other garlic clove and add to the bowl with half the orange and lemon zest. Mix well and leave to stand for 1 hour.

3   Mince the pork fat once through the finest blade of your mincer and repeat with the meat, passing it through twice. Combine the two in a chilled bowl, then pass this forcemeat through a sieve.

4   Heat the remaining 3 tbsp oil in a frying pan over a high heat. Season the pheasant breasts and quickly seal them on both sides in the hot oil. Remove and set aside.

5   Melt the butter in the pan and cook the shallots until softened. Add the brandy and reduced stock, bring to the boil and skim. Add 4 juniper berries, the remaining citrus zest and some pepper and reduce to a thick liquor. Allow to cool.

6   Preheat the oven to 170°C/Gas 3. Mix the pistachios into the forcemeat. Line a terrine with the pork fat slices and add one-third of the forcemeat, pushing it well into the corners. Add the sealed pheasant breasts and brush with the reduction. Cover with the remaining forcemeat. Fold over the excess fat and cover with another layer of fat.

7   Cover the terrine with cling film, then foil, and stand in a roasting tin containing enough hot water to come halfway up the sides. Cook in the oven for 1 hour 20 minutes, making sure the water remains at a simmer.

8   Remove from the water bath and allow to cool, then press with a light weight and leave to mature in the fridge for 5 days before eating.

POULTRY

I can assure you that if you go that extra mile to buy a quality chicken, or any other well-bred bird for that matter, you will certainly taste the difference. I get mine from a small farm that is registered with the Soil Association. There is a very low number of birds to each hen house and they are fed on a GM free diet. Their superior living conditions and diet is reflected in the flavour of the meat. You only have do a bit of research to realise that the way most chickens are reared in this country is not only cruel on the birds, but also on the flavour of the meat they produce. So stay away from cheap mass-produced poultry!

Firstly, make sure you know where the chicken or other bird(s) you are buying comes from. Freshness is very important, so check that the bird is well within its 'use-by' date. It should have good, firm flesh and skin that is unblemished and intact. Store in the fridge for no longer than 2 days before cooking.

There are so many dishes you can prepare using chicken, because it lends itself to practically any flavour or style of cooking. Poach, roast, grill, fry, bake or casserole – chicken will work well with any method. My favourite part of a roast chicken is the winglets because I love the crispy chicken skin and the fibrous muscle tissue underneath.

If there is any leftover chicken from our Sunday roast, I dice up the meat, stir it into mashed potato with little florets of broccoli and shape the mixture into patties, like burgers. I dip them in seasoned flour, then into beaten egg and finally into large breadcrumbs before shallow-frying in oil until golden. My kids love these for supper!

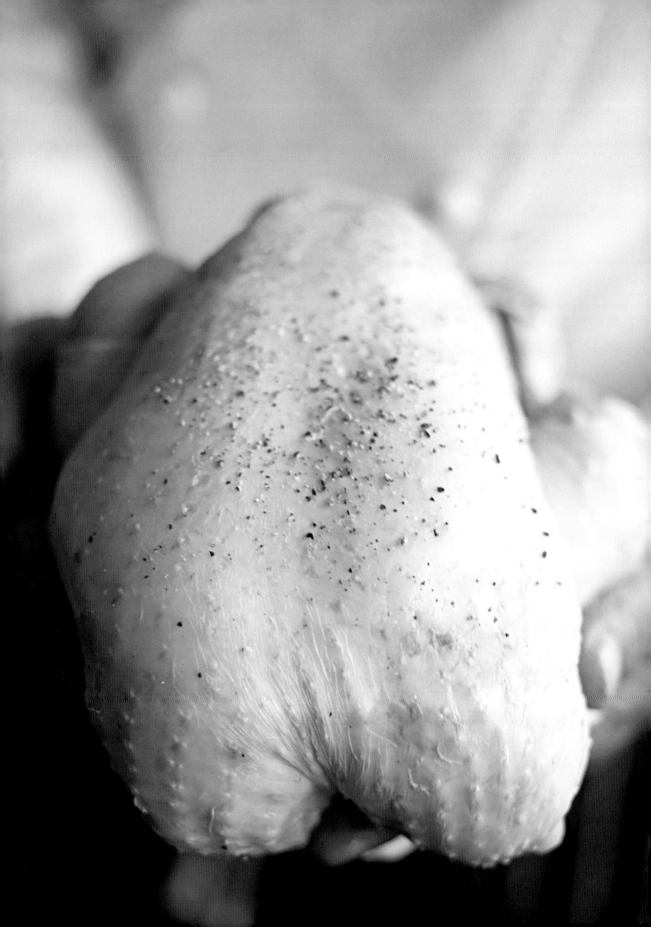

ROAST CHICKEN WITH A LEMON, THYME AND GARLIC BUTTER

Stuffing a zesty flavoured butter beneath the skin of the chicken helps to keep the meat moist in the oven and really enhances the flavour of the roast. Serve with steamed or braised cabbage and roasted or sauté potatoes.

1.8kg oven-ready chicken (either organic or free-range)

1 lemon

100g unsalted butter, softened

1 garlic clove, peeled and crushed

salt and pepper

3 thyme sprigs, leaves stripped (stalks reserved)

4 SERVINGS

1   Preheat the oven to 230°C/Gas 8. Lay the chicken on its side and press down to crack the rib bones and release the gelatinous juices – these help to flavour and thicken the gravy. Working from the neck end, loosen the skin over the breast to make space for the butter.

2   Grate the zest from the lemon and mix into the softened butter with the garlic, salt, pepper and thyme leaves. Push the butter under the chicken skin and squash it down so that it covers the breast completely.

3   Halve the lemon, squeeze the juice and stuff the halves into the cavity of the chicken along with the lemon juice and thyme stalks. Season the chicken with salt and pepper and place in a roasting tray. Roast in the oven for 10–15 minutes.

4   Baste the chicken with the cooking juices, then lower the oven setting to 190°C/Gas 5. Roast, basting from time to time, for a further 50–55 minutes or until the chicken is cooked. To test, pierce the thickest part of the thigh with a skewer – the juices should run clear, not at all pink.

5   Transfer the chicken to a warmed platter and cover with foil. Leave in a warm spot to rest for 15 minutes. Return the roasting tray to the heat, add 150ml water and bring to the boil, scraping up the sediment to deglaze the pan and incorporate the cooking juices. Season and pour into a jug.

6   Carve the chicken and serve with the gravy and vegetables of your choice.

CHICKEN AND ROOT VEGETABLE CASSEROLE

This is a great one-pot-dish that's good for those winter Sunday nights in front of the fire. Served with a garlicky tarragon mayo and crusty French bread, it is real comfort food.

1.6kg oven-ready chicken (corn-fed or organic)

2 celery sticks

1 large leek, washed

2 large carrots, peeled

2 large potatoes, peeled and washed

1 large onion, peeled

2 tarragon sprigs

1 rosemary sprig

2 thyme sprigs

1 bay leaf

2 flat leaf parsley sprigs

2 garlic cloves, peeled and crushed

10 black peppercorns, crushed

50g fresh horseradish root, peeled and thinly sliced

4 lemon slices

200ml white wine

1 litre chicken stock (see page 247)

salt and pepper

TO SERVE

garlic and tarragon mayonnaise (see page 250)

4 SERVINGS

1 Joint the chicken into eight pieces. First cut the legs off and divide in two (thigh and drumstick). Then cut down either side of the backbone and remove it. Cut each breast into two pieces. (Save the bones and trimmings to make stock.) Place the chicken in a flameproof casserole or cooking pot and set aside.

2 Cut the celery, leek and carrots into 4cm lengths. Cut the potatoes and onion into 4cm dice. Place all the vegetables in the casserole with the chicken.

3 Add the herbs, garlic, black peppercorns, horseradish, lemon slices, white wine and stock. Bring slowly to the boil and skim off any scum that rises to the surface. Lower the heat and simmer gently for approximately 1 hour, skimming occasionally.

4 Transfer the chicken and vegetables to a warmed serving dish. Boil the stock to reduce slightly, check the seasoning and ladle over the chicken. Serve with the garlic and tarragon mayonnaise and plenty of warm crusty bread.

HOT CHICKEN LIVER PARFAIT

This parfait is simple to make and very tasty. It works equally well with duck livers, if you are able to get hold of some. Serve as a starter with hot toast and gherkins. You will need to marinate the livers and prepare the ramekins a day ahead.

300g chicken livers

1 small garlic clove, peeled and crushed

1 tbsp Madeira

1 tbsp port

pinch of freshly grated nutmeg

salt and pepper

75g unsalted butter, melted

3 large eggs

3 egg yolks

125ml double cream

300ml milk

few drops of lemon juice

TO SERVE

hot buttered toast

gherkins

6 SERVINGS

1   The evening before, trim the livers, cutting away any green coloured parts (as these are bitter). Put the livers in a small bowl and add the garlic, Madeira and port. Season with nutmeg, salt and pepper. Cover and put in the fridge to marinate overnight.

2   Generously brush 6 ramekins, measuring 7cm wide and 4cm deep, with 60g of the butter. Turn them upside down on a tray and refrigerate for 5 minutes or until the butter has set. Leave in the fridge until required.

3   The next day, tip the contents of the bowl of chicken livers into a blender. Add the whole eggs, egg yolks, cream, milk, lemon juice and remaining melted butter. Season with a little salt and pepper and blitz the mixture until smooth. Strain through a fine sieve into a bowl, pressing the mixture through with the back of a ladle.

4   Preheat the oven to 170°C/Gas 3. Half-fill a roasting tray with almost boiling water. Take the buttered ramekins out of the fridge and line the base of each one with a disc of greaseproof paper. Fill with the parfait mixture and carefully stand them in the roasting tray (the water level should be 5mm below the rims). Take a sheet of greaseproof paper and make some slits to allow the steam to escape. Wet the paper under cold running water, shake off excess and lay over the mousses. Carefully place in the oven and cook for about 40 minutes until set.

5   Take the ramekins out of the water, run a knife around the inside of each one and invert on to a serving plate. Carefully shake the mousses free.

6   Serve at once, with hot toast and gherkins.

ROAST QUAIL WITH WARM RADISH AND MOLASSES BUTTER

This is a lovely light lunch – delicious served with sautéed pak choi or a leafy salad. For a more substantial main course, serve two quails per person and double the quantity of rice.

4 quails, wishbones
    removed
salt and pepper
3 tbsp oil
60g basmati rice
60g butter
15g molasses or dark
    muscovado sugar
finely pared zest of
    1 orange
1cm piece cinnamon stick
1 star anise
24 radishes, trimmed and
    halved
2 tsp chopped chives

4 SERVINGS

1   Preheat the oven to 220°C/Gas 7. Season the quails with salt and pepper. Heat 1–2 tbsp oil in a heavy-based ovenproof pan. Brown them in the hot oil – first on one leg, then the other and finally on the breast. Turn the birds on to their backs and place in the hot oven for 6 minutes. The quail should be pink and underdone. Allow to cool.

2   Meanwhile, cook the rice in boiling salted water until tender, about 15 minutes. In another pan, slowly melt 40g of the butter and mix in the molasses or sugar. Heat gently until combined. Set aside.

3   Using a sharp knife, cut away each quail leg, then following the breastbone, carefully ease away each breast in one piece, cutting through the wing bone joint. You will have four pieces from each quail – two legs and two breasts.

4   Drain the rice as soon as it is cooked, rinse under boiling water, then add the orange zest, cinnamon and star anise. Season if necessary.

5   When ready to serve, warm a pan big enough to hold all the quail. Add a splash of oil and add the quail pieces, breasts skin side down, legs skin side up. Pour in the molasses butter and move the pieces about in the warm mixture coating them well.

6   Heat a little oil in a separate pan over a medium heat. Add the radishes, toss slowly and season with salt and pepper. Add a knob of butter and allow to melt. Sprinkle in the chives. Meanwhile, gently reheat the rice if necessary.

7   Spoon the rice into the centre of warmed plates, discarding the flavourings. Arrange the quail pieces on top and spoon over some molasses butter. Surround with the warm radishes and spoon a little of the molasses butter around the plates. Serve at once.

POUSSIN WITH CURRY AND LIME

Get your butcher to 'crown' the poussins for you and ask him to give you the legs and some chicken bones (for the sauce). You will need to marinate the poussins a day in advance.

3 medium poussins

450g chicken bones

8 shallots, peeled

½ carrot, peeled

1 leek, washed

½ celery stick

6 tbsp vegetable oil

1 garlic clove, smashed

600ml chicken stock
   (see page 247)

1 thyme sprig

bunch of spring onions

180g peanuts, shelled

salt and pepper

180ml double cream

MARINADE

juice of 4 oranges

juice of 2 limes

2 red chillies, deseeded
   and chopped

30g fresh root ginger,
   peeled and grated

1 garlic clove, smashed

1 tbsp curry powder

110ml olive oil

40g fresh coconut flesh,
   grated, plus 100ml liquid

1 thyme sprig

2 tbsp soy sauce

60g demerara sugar

6 SERVINGS

1   Combine the marinade ingredients in a large bowl, stir well and add the poussin crowns and legs. Turn to coat, then cover and marinate in the fridge for 24 hours.

2   The next day, chop the chicken bones, shallots, carrot, leek and celery. Heat half the oil in a large saucepan until smoking. Fry the bones until golden brown, then add the chopped vegetables, lower the heat and cook until golden.

3   Drain the marinade from the poussins and pour it over the bones and vegetables. Add the garlic, stock and thyme. Bring to the boil, skim, then simmer for 30 minutes.

4   Trim and finely shred the spring onions and set aside. Dry roast the peanuts in a pan until golden, season with salt and set aside.

5   Preheat the oven to 220°C/Gas 7. Heat the remaining 3 tbsp oil in a heavy-based frying pan. Season the poussin pieces and carefully brown on all sides. Transfer to a roasting tray and roast for 10 minutes until the breasts are tender. Remove the breasts and carry on roasting the legs for an extra 5–10 minutes. Take the breasts off the bone and keep warm, along with the legs.

6   Strain the sauce through a muslin-lined sieve into a clean pan and bubble to reduce by half, skimming often. Put a ladleful of the sauce into another pan and reduce this more quickly until sticky, then add 60ml of cream. When it comes to the boil, add the shredded spring onions, mix well and season. Baste the poussin pieces with the spring onion mixture and place in the oven for a few minutes to reheat.

7   Add the remaining cream to the reducing sauce and boil rapidly to a creamy consistency. Check the seasoning.

8   Arrange the poussin pieces and spring onions on a bed of basmati rice. Spoon the sauce around the chicken, sprinkle over the roasted peanuts and serve immediately.

ROAST DUCK WITH CHERRIES IN BANYULS WINE

One of my favourite places in France is Céret, home to the best cherries on the planet. Close by, on the terrace vineyards overlooking the Mediterranean near Collioure, the grapes that produce sweet Banyuls wine are grown. Here I use them together to cut the richness of fatty roast duck. It is a delicious dish and one of my all-time favourites.

2 small organic or free-range Barbary ducks, 4–5kg in total

salt and pepper

1 onion, peeled and chopped

1 large carrot, peeled and chopped

2 celery sticks, trimmed and chopped

2 garlic cloves, peeled and crushed

1 bay leaf

1 thyme sprig

1 jar poached cherries in Banyuls wine (see page 225)

200ml red wine

750ml chicken stock (see page 247)

watercress sprigs, to garnish

4 SERVINGS

1   Preheat the oven to 230°C/Gas 8. Season the ducks with salt and pepper and place in a large roasting tin. Roast in the oven for 40–45 minutes. Transfer to a wire rack to cool. Pour off the fat from the roasting tin and reserve. When cool, remove the legs and breasts from the ducks (they will be very rare at this stage) and return to the roasting tin; set aside. Chop up the carcasses and reserve.

2   Heat all except 1 tbsp of the duck fat in a large frying pan or roasting tin until it is almost smoking, then add the duck bones and lightly brown all over, turning frequently. Add the chopped vegetables, lower the heat and cook until softened and golden. Add the garlic and herbs and cook for about 1 minute.

3   Drain the juice from the bottled cherries and pour half of it into a large saucepan. Add the browned duck bones and vegetables, then pour in the red wine. Bring to the boil and reduce by two-thirds.

4   Add half of the cherries and the stock and bring to the boil. Skim, then simmer for 45 minutes or until the sauce has reduced by half. Strain the sauce through a fine sieve into a clean pan, add the remaining cherries and check the seasoning. Set aside.

5   Roast the duck legs and breasts for a further 8–10 minutes or until tender and pink. Arrange the duck on a warmed serving platter and spoon over some of the sauce and cherries. Garnish with sprigs of watercress and serve with pak choi or Swiss chard and rösti (see page 44) or mashed potatoes. Hand the remaining sauce around separately in a jug.

WILD DUCK BREAST AND AUTUMN FRUITS WITH AN ARMAGNAC SAUCE

3 wild ducks (mallards),
   plucked and drawn
3 tbsp vegetable oil
110ml red wine vinegar
1 tbsp redcurrant jelly
10 juniper berries, crushed
finely pared zest and juice
   of 1 orange
1 onion, peeled and
   roughly chopped
½ carrot, peeled and
   roughly chopped
1 leek, washed and
   roughly chopped
1 celery stick, roughly
   chopped
6 garlic cloves, peeled
1 thyme sprig
1 bay leaf
60ml port
90ml Armagnac
1.2 litres chicken stock
   (see page 247)
90g cranberries (optional)
1–2 tbsp sugar, plus extra
   to sprinkle
salt and pepper
1–2 pears, peeled, cored
   and sliced
30g butter
3 figs, quartered

6 SERVINGS

1   Take out the wish bone and carefully remove the legs from the ducks, without cutting into the breast meat. Turn the bird breast down and carefully snip away the backbone. Cover the duck breasts and refrigerate until needed.

2   Chop up the bones and legs (these are tough and have little meat). Heat 2 tbsp oil in a roasting pan until almost smoking, add the bones and brown all over, turning often.

3   Meanwhile, in a large heavy-based saucepan, heat the wine vinegar, redcurrant jelly, juniper and orange zest and reduce to a thick syrup. Add the roasted bones and turn until well glazed. Brown the chopped vegetables in the roasting pan, then add to the bones with the garlic and herbs.

4   In a small pan, heat the port and Armagnac. Ignite and burn off the alcohol, then add to the bones and pour in the stock. Bring to the boil, skim and simmer for 45 minutes.

5   Slowly bring the orange juice to the boil in another pan, skim and add two-thirds to the simmering stock. Poach the cranberries in the remainder with a little sugar until tender. Taste for sweetness, adding more sugar if needed.

6   Preheat the oven to 220°C/Gas 7. Heat 1 tbsp oil in a roasting pan. Season the duck breasts and sear them, skin side down, in the hot pan for about 3 minutes until golden brown. Transfer to the oven and cook for a further 8–12 minutes depending on size, until tender and still pink. Meanwhile, strain the stock into a clean pan and boil to reduce by half. Pass through a muslin-lined sieve.

7   Rest the duck breasts for 5 minutes. Sprinkle the pears with pepper and sugar and cook in a hot pan with the butter until golden. Warm the figs in a little sweetened water.

8   Cut the duck breasts off the bone and pull off the skin. Cover with foil and keep warm. Roll up the skin, slice thinly, season and place on a tray in the oven to crisp up.

9   Slice the duck and arrange on warmed plates with the fruit. Spoon over the sauce, top with the crisp skin and serve.

FRUIT

APPLES

These are well suited to our climate and there are far more homegrown varieties than you'd imagine from the limited range in supermarkets. Visit Appledore in Kent and you'll find a living monument of 1000 native species! The paltry choice of apples in our shops is a disappointment to me, though living in the southwest I am luckier than most, as apples are vital to the local cider industry.

Choosing the right apples for cooking is important. Bramley's are our best-loved cooking apple. They have a fine flavour and turn pulpy on cooking, which is ideal for sauces and alike, but I often use dessert apples in cooking. Here you need to be careful with the apples you choose, because most varieties are too soft-fleshed and not acidic enough to maintain their flavour. Granny Smiths are a good choice, as they are tart and hold their shape well during cooking.

When buying any apples, choose ones that are firm and free from wrinkles and blemishes. Apples keep well – even imported fruit, which gives us year round availability, though I would advise you to make the most of homegrown apples as they come into season.

Apart from being delicious to eat raw, apples are used in numerous dessert recipes, especially pies, tarts and baked puddings. They work incredibly well in many savoury dishes too. I use apples with duck dishes in the same way as I use them with roast pork. And apple is great diced into a curry, or chopped finely into a steamed mussel dish, or served as an accompaniment to salmon with horseradish cream. As far as I am concerned, their versatility is second to none.

BAKED APPLES WITH PRUNES AND WALNUTS

Served with crème anglaise (see page 251), this is a lovely, simple autumnal dessert. You can also serve these apples as a garnish to roast pork.

3 Granny Smith apples

15g ready-to-eat prunes, chopped

100g shelled walnuts, chopped

50g unsalted butter, softened

2 tbsp soft brown sugar (preferably muscovado)

6 SERVINGS

1   Preheat the oven to 200°C/Gas 6. Halve the apples horizontally and scoop out the core, using a melon baller, without cutting through, to form a cavity for the filling.

2   In a bowl, mix the prunes and walnuts with the soft butter, then use to fill the apple cavities, packing it in and piling it up well. Sprinkle with the sugar. Place the apples on a baking tray and bake in the oven for 6–8 minutes until they have started to soften and the butter has melted. Preheat the grill, meanwhile.

3   Place the tray of apples under the grill until the sugar is caramelised and golden brown, about 3 minutes. Leave to stand for about 5 minutes before serving.

APPLE AND TARRAGON COMPOTE

This compote is an excellent accompaniment to pork and cold meats. It is best served at room temperature.

6 Granny Smith apples

20g unsalted butter

3 tarragon sprigs, blanched (briefly in boiling water) drained and chopped

1–2 tsp soft brown sugar (preferably muscovado)

4–6 SERVINGS

1   Peel, core and roughly chop the apples. Melt the butter in a sauté pan over a low heat, add the apples and cook for about 6–8 minutes or until they start to release their juice. Cover and cook very slowly, stirring occasionally to prevent sticking, for a further 10–12 minutes or until the apples are just tender but still holding their shape. Take off the heat.

2   Add the tarragon and fork through, keeping the apple pieces fairly chunky. Sweeten with a little sugar to taste and leave to cool before serving.

TARTE NORMANDE

Use the best butter that you can afford to make the pastry for this tart – it will make all the difference. The tart is equally good hot, warm or at room temperature, served with crème fraîche, crème anglaise (see page 251) or cream.

PASTRY
220g plain flour, plus
   extra for dusting
generous pinch of salt
100g butter, diced

FILLING
6 apples (preferably Cox's
   Orange Pippins)
90ml whipping cream
3 egg yolks
1 tbsp caster sugar
pinch of ground
   cinnamon
pinch of salt
finely grated zest of
   1 lemon

TO FINISH
30g butter, diced
3 tbsp caster sugar
icing sugar, for dusting

8 SERVINGS

1 To make the pastry, sift the flour and salt into a bowl, add the butter and rub into the flour, using your fingertips until you have a crumbly consistency. Gradually mix in enough water (about 4–5 tbsp) to bind the mixture, using a round-bladed knife. When the dough begins to come together, gather with your hand and knead gently until the pastry forms a ball. Wrap in cling film and rest in the fridge for 30 minutes.

2 Roll the pastry out on a lightly floured surface to a 5mm thickness and use to line a 25cm tart tin. Leave to rest in the fridge, loosely covered with cling film.

3 Preheat the oven to 200°C/Gas 6. Peel the apples, then cut them into large segments, removing the core and pips. In a bowl, whisk together the cream, egg yolks, sugar, cinnamon, salt and lemon zest.

4 Arrange the apple segments evenly in the pastry case and pour the creamy mixture over them. Place the tart tin on a baking sheet and bake for 30 minutes.

5 Take out of the oven and dot the butter over the surface. Sprinkle with the 3 tbsp sugar and return to the oven for 5 minutes or until golden and caramelised. Dust with icing sugar to serve.

PEARS

At their peak, pears are sweet and juicy, lending themselves brilliantly to many desserts. There are numerous varieties, ranging from green, through yellow to red pears, some with smooth skins, others speckled or russeted, though you're unlikely to find more than a handful of these in the shops. My favourite variety is Williams – delicious as a dessert fruit, but also when cooked because it holds its texture and flavour well. Conference pears are less flavoursome and, in my opinion, best used in chutneys.

As with other delicate fruit, you need to buy pears when they are in season and when ripe, but firm. Here, the first pear crops ripen in July, but this fruit is at its best during the autumn months. Choose pears that feel firm, but not hard. The colour will depend on the variety, but Williams pears should be yellow with speckled skin.

Compared with apples, pears are far more temperamental and don't keep very well after they have been picked. There is a very small 'window' of perfect ripeness, which you need to catch, because after this the flavour and texture deteriorate quickly. Bear this in mind when you are buying pears – little and often is the key – otherwise you'll probably experience a lot of wastage.

In cooking, the flavour of pears can be enhanced by other ingredients such as almonds, walnuts and vanilla. Poached in red wine or a liqueur flavoured syrup, they are delicious and I adore pears with chocolate – the two really complement each other. Pears are also great with cheese, especially a tasty block of Stilton.

PEARS POACHED IN POIRE WILLIAM

8 medium ripe, but firm
    pears (preferably
    Williams or Packham)
juice of ¹/₂ lemon
800g caster sugar
2 vanilla pods, split
200ml Poire William eau
    de vie liqueur

8 SERVINGS

1   Peel the pears and scoop out the core from the base, but keep the stalk intact. Roll in lemon juice to stop browning.
2   Put the sugar, vanilla pods and 1.3 litres water in a heavy-based pan (which will hold the pears). Heat slowly to dissolve the sugar, bring to the boil and add the liqueur.
3   Add the pears, cover with greaseproof paper and lay a heatproof plate on top to keep them submerged in the syrup. Cook over a low heat for 10–15 minutes or until soft. Take off the heat and leave the pears to cool in the syrup.
4   Once cool, you can bottle the pears in their syrup in sterilised jars and store in the fridge for up to 6 months. They are delicious in tarts or served simply with ice cream.

GINGER CREME CARAMEL WITH GRILLED PEAR

100g caster sugar, plus
    extra to sprinkle
4 ripe Williams pears,
    peeled, cored and sliced

CUSTARD
500ml milk
1 piece preserved stem
    ginger, finely chopped
100g caster sugar
3 eggs, plus 1 egg yolk

4 SERVINGS

1   Preheat the oven to 170°C/Gas 3. For the custard, slowly heat the milk with the ginger and half the sugar in a pan. Beat the eggs, yolk and remaining sugar in a bowl. When almost boiling, whisk in the hot milk, then strain into a jug.
2   For the caramel, dissolve the 100g sugar in 6 tbsp water in a small heavy-based pan, then boil to a light caramel. Pour into 4 ramekins or dariole moulds and swirl to coat the bases. Allow to set, then pour in the custard
3   Stand in a roasting tray containing enough water to come halfway up the sides. Cover with greaseproof paper and bake for 40–50 minutes until set. Remove and let cool.
4   Preheat the grill. Peel, core and slice the pears, dredge with sugar and grill until the pear slices start to caramelise.
5   Run a knife around the edge of each crème caramel and turn out on to a plate. Add the hot pear slices and serve.

PEAR TARTS WITH CHOCOLATE SORBET

I love to serve these beautiful tarts topped with a scoop of chocolate sorbet, but you can simply serve them with a scoop of vanilla ice cream, or with crème anglaise (see page 251).

400g ready-made puff
    pastry
flour, for dusting
6 large pears, poached in
    Poire William (see page
    207), drained
icing sugar, to dust

FRANGIPANE

100g unsalted butter
100g caster sugar
2 eggs
100g ground almonds
10g plain flour
2 tsp amaretto liqueur

**CHOCOLATE SORBET
(OPTIONAL)**

250ml milk
150g caster sugar
50g liquid glucose
200g dark chocolate
    (at least 70% cocoa
    solids), in pieces

6 SERVINGS

1   If serving the sorbet, make this first. Pour the milk and 250ml water into a pan, add the sugar and liquid glucose and heat slowly to dissolve the sugar. Bring to the boil and take off the heat. Add the chocolate and stir continuously until it has melted completely. Skim off any scum from the surface, then pass through a fine sieve into a bowl and leave to cool completely. When the mixture is cold, transfer to an ice-cream machine – or sorbetière – and churn until smooth and frozen.

2   For the tarts, roll out the puff pastry on a lightly floured surface to a 4–5 mm thickness. Cut out six 12cm discs, using an inverted plate as a guide. Prick the discs all over with a fork and place on a tray. Cover loosely with cling film and rest in the fridge while you prepare the filling.

3   For the frangipane, beat the butter and sugar together in a bowl until creamy and pale in colour. Beat in the eggs, one at a time. Next, add the ground almonds and flour and mix until smooth. Finally, stir in the liqueur. Preheat the oven to 220°C/Gas 7.

4   Transfer the pastry discs to a baking sheet and place a sheet of baking parchment on top. Lay another baking tray on top (to weigh down) and bake for 8–10 minutes or until golden brown and crisp. Set aside to cool.

5   Cut the pears in half and slice very thinly, keeping their shape. Drain on kitchen paper. Spread a layer of frangipane over each pastry disc, about 2mm thick. Arrange the pear slices on top, to cover all the pastry and frangipane. Bake for 5–6 minutes until golden and warmed through.

6   Place a pear tart on each warmed plate and top with a scoop of chocolate sorbet if serving. Dust with icing sugar and serve immediately.

PLUMS

These come in a variety of colours and sizes, but the different plums are largely interchangeable in cooking. Just make the most of each kind as it comes into season and don't miss out on beautiful greengages, damsons and small Mirabelle plums if you are lucky enough to come across them. Some plums will have a higher sugar content than others, so you may need to adjust the amount of sugar in a recipe to allow for this. Dried plums – or prunes – are also wonderful in cooking, lending an intense sweet taste of the fruit. Juicy Agen prunes are especially good.

Late summer is, of course, the time to enjoy plums, when homegrown fruit becomes available. Personally, I wouldn't dream of buying them in winter as they would have been picked while green, transported hundreds of miles and will have little, if any, flavour.

Plums are delicate, so you need to choose them carefully, picking out fruits that are firm, smooth and unblemished. They should also be fully coloured for their variety. Plums don't keep well, so buy only as many as you will consume within 2 or 3 days.

Plums are excellent in pies, crumbles and many other desserts, as well as preserves. If you happen to have a damson tree in the garden, you'll probably find they ripen all at once, so use them to make jam. Plums also go extremely well with fatty meats, as they cut the richness. For example, I like to use them in a stuffing for goose or as a sauce to go with roast duck. Try adding some fresh plums to a beef casserole for a new twist, or make a spiced plum chutney to serve with gammon.

PLUM CLAFOUTIS

This traditional French dessert works well with other fruits, notably fresh cherries, apricots and little green Mirabelle plums. If preferred, you can omit the pastry case and bake the clafoutis mixture in a buttered gratin dish.

SWEET PASTRY

150g unsalted butter, plus
    extra to grease
50g icing sugar
1 egg
250g plain flour, plus
    extra for dusting

FILLING

200ml whipping cream
½ vanilla pod
4 eggs
50g caster sugar
15 plums

6 SERVINGS

1 Grease and flour a 25cm tart tin. To make the pastry, beat the butter and icing sugar together in a bowl until light and fluffy. Add the egg and continue to beat until the mixture is smooth. Work in the flour until you have a smooth dough that comes away from the side of the bowl. Turn out on to a lightly floured surface, knead gently and shape into a ball. Wrap in cling film and leave to rest in the fridge for 2 hours.

2 Preheat the oven to 200°C/Gas 6. Roll out the pastry on a lightly floured surface to a thickness of 5mm and use to line the prepared tin. Place on a baking sheet. Line the pastry case with greaseproof paper and baking beans and bake blind for 10 minutes. Remove the beans and paper and bake for a further 5 minutes. Set aside while you prepare the filling. Lower the oven setting to 170°C/Gas 3.

3 For the filling, pour the cream into a pan. Split open the vanilla pod to expose the seeds and add to the pan. Slowly bring to the boil, then remove from the heat and set aside to infuse.

4 Meanwhile, beat the eggs and caster sugar together lightly. When the cream is just warm, pour on to the eggs and sugar, whisking constantly. Strain through a fine sieve into a jug.

5 Halve the plums and remove the stones, then arrange over the base of the pastry case. Carefully pour the cream mixture over the top. Bake in the oven for 20 minutes until golden. Serve warm, with crème anglaise (see page 251).

PRUNE AND ARMAGNAC TART

This tart is one of my favourites, so I had to include it here... and prunes are dried plums, after all! Select good quality prunes, such as Agen, for optimum flavour.

150g prunes

2 tbsp Armagnac (or Cognac)

30g plum jam

20g flaked almonds

SWEET PASTRY

100g unsalted butter

100g icing sugar

1 egg

200g plain flour, plus extra for dusting

melted butter, for brushing

ALMOND CREAM

100g unsalted butter

100g caster sugar

2 eggs

100g ground almonds

10g cornflour

TO FINISH

60g icing sugar

6 SERVINGS

1   Wash the prunes, drain and remove the stones, using a sharp small knife. Put them in a small bowl, sprinkle with the Armagnac and leave to soak overnight.

2   To make the pastry, beat the butter and icing sugar together in a bowl until soft and pale. Beat in the egg and then fold in the flour to make a smooth dough. Knead gently, then shape into a ball. Wrap in cling film and leave to rest in the fridge for 1 hour.

3   Roll out the pastry on a lightly floured surface to a 5mm thickness. Place a 3cm deep, 28cm flan ring on a baking sheet and lightly brush the inside with butter. Line the flan ring with the pastry, trim off excess and prick the base with a fork. Cover loosely with cling film and rest in the fridge for 20 minutes. Preheat the oven to 200°C/Gas 6.

4   For the almond cream, beat the butter and caster sugar together in a bowl until pale and fluffy. Add the eggs, one at a time, beating well. Add the ground almonds and cornflour and continue beating for at least 5 minutes.

5   Line the pastry case with greaseproof paper and baking beans and bake blind for 10 minutes. Remove the beans and paper and bake for a further 5 minutes. Allow to cool.

6   Spread the plum jam over the pastry base, then spoon the almond cream evenly on top. Drain the prunes over a bowl to save the juices. Scatter the prunes over the almond cream and press them in. Top with the flaked almonds and bake for about 35–40 minutes until golden brown.

7   Remove the tart from the oven and set aside to cool. Mix the icing sugar with 2 tbsp of the reserved prune juices to make a thick syrup. Brush over the top of the cooled tart and carefully remove the flan ring. Serve the tart with hot crème anglaise (see page 251).

DAMSON JAM

If you have a glut of damsons or plums in the garden, don't let them go to waste. Turn them into jam and you can enjoy their flavour all year round. Spread on to fresh bread or toast for a delicious breakfast or spoon on to muffins, scones or toasted crumpets at teatime.

1kg damsons or wild plums
1kg granulated sugar, warmed

MAKES ABOUT 2KG

1 Put the damsons into a preserving pan or other large enough heavy-based pan and add 1.4 litres cold water. Slowly bring to the boil and skim off any scum from the surface, then lower the heat to a simmer. Cook for about 10–15 minutes until the damsons are soft and the liquid has reduced down.

2 When the fruit is soft, add the warmed sugar and stir until it has totally dissolved. Bring the mixture to the boil, skimming out any stones that rise to the surface. Carry on boiling, stirring frequently, until the jam reaches its setting point and registers 105°C on a sugar thermometer. To test for a set, spoon a little of the jam on to a cold saucer and push your finger across it. If the surface wrinkles and it is beginning to set, it is ready.

3 Once the jam has reached setting point, take off the heat and set aside to cool for about 10 minutes.

4 Pour the jam into sterilised jars, filling them almost to the top and cover the surface with a waxed disc while still hot. Leave to go cold, then cover the jars with cellophane and secure with an elastic band. Label and store in a cool, dark place for up to 6 months.

5 Refrigerate the jam after opening.

NOTE To sterilise jars, wash thoroughly in very hot soapy water, rinse well, then place upside down on a baking tray in the oven at 140°C/Gas 1 for 10–15 minutes until completely dry. Place, still upturned, on a clean tea towel until the jam is ready for potting.

APRICOTS

Like peaches and nectarines, apricots have a very distinctive flavour, but to really appreciate their fragrant quality you need to eat them when they are perfectly ripe. The natural ripening process stops as soon as they are taken from the tree, so apricots that are picked under-ripe and transported from afar are usually very disappointing. The best apricots that I have ever tasted came from the Loire Valley in France.

Apricots are not particularly abundant in this country because they rely on plenty of sunshine, but as our summers become warmer, they are increasingly available. During their short season, from June to August, I always look to buy apricots at their peak and bottle them in liqueur-flavoured syrups, so I can enjoy them beyond their season. I also use dried apricots in my recipes, as I regard them to be the best of all dried fruits, because they maintain their flavour so well.

When choosing apricots, look for fruit with a soft pink, matt blush that are tender, but not overly soft. They should have a distinct, sweet aroma. Eat within a few days of purchase, otherwise you will find that the fruit quickly softens – especially if kept in a fruit bowl alongside other ripe fruits.

I use apricots in numerous desserts, especially in combination with almonds as their flavours complement each other so well. Apricots are also brilliant in savoury dishes, especially with lamb. And as a change from grapes, serve freshly sliced apricots with a cheese board – their slight tartness counteracts the richness of creamy cheeses perfectly.

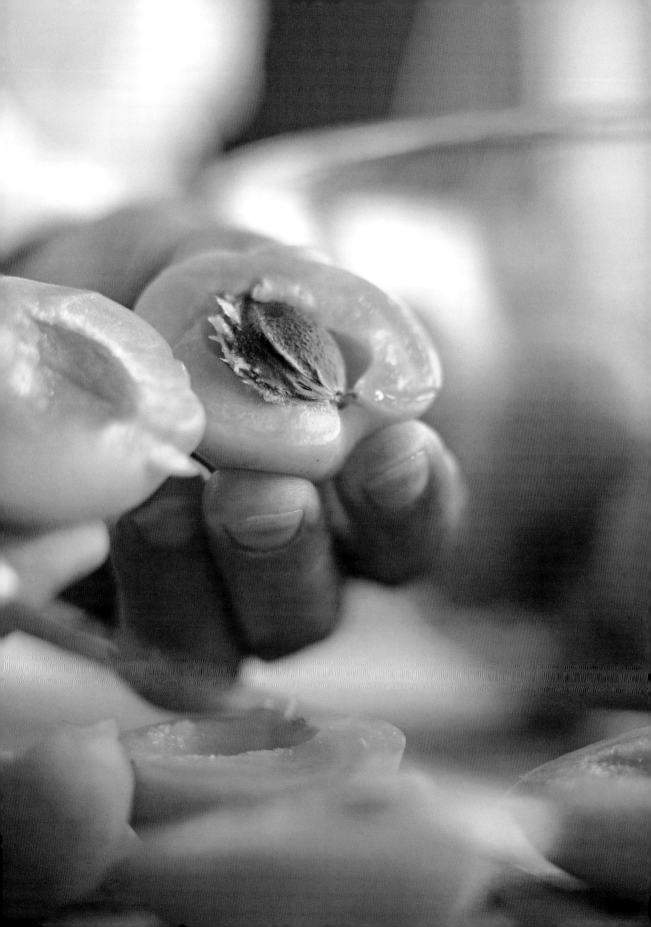

APRICOTS IN AMARETTO SYRUP

This is an excellent way to prepare apricots in the height of their season. They are delicious with ice cream or sorbet and lend themselves to many delectable desserts. The apricots will keep for up to 6 months if sealed properly, but once opened, they should be eaten right away.

1.3kg firm, ripe apricots
800g granulated sugar
1 vanilla pod, split, seeds
  removed
175ml amaretto liqueur

6 SERVINGS

1   Cut a slit in each apricot and remove the stone, keeping the fruit as whole as possible. Place in a suitable pan.

2   Pour 1 litre water into a heavy-based pan and add half the sugar and the empty vanilla pod. Heat gently until the sugar dissolves, then increase the heat and simmer for 5 minutes.

3   Add the apricots and simmer for 3–4 minutes or until just tender, but still holding their shape. Drain the apricots in a sieve over a bowl to save the syrup.

4   Return the sugar syrup to the pan and add the remaining sugar. Slowly bring to the boil to dissolve the sugar, then boil until the syrup registers 104°C on a sugar thermometer.

5   Remove the pan from the heat and allow the sugar syrup to cool slightly. Discard the vanilla pod, then add the amaretto liquor.

6   Pack the apricots into warmed, sterilised jars and pour the warm syrup over them, tilting and tapping the jars to expel any air. Seal and store in a cool, dark place for 2 weeks before using, to allow time for the flavour to develop.

APRICOT SABAYON

1 jar apricots in amaretto
   syrup (see page 219)
8 egg yolks
80g caster sugar
60g flaked almonds
2 tsp icing sugar

4–6 SERVINGS

1   Preheat the grill to high. Drain the jar of apricots in a sieve over a bowl to save the syrup. Set aside.

2   Put the egg yolks and caster sugar in a large heatproof bowl and add 300ml of the syrup from the apricots. Place the bowl over a pan of simmering water and whisk at maximum speed for 5 minutes until the mixture turns pale and starts to thicken.

3   Carry on whisking for a further 5 minutes or until the sabayon is thick and creamy. Take the bowl off the pan and whisk as the sabayon cools, until it's barely warm.

4   Preheat the grill. Arrange the apricot halves on heatproof plates and spoon the sabayon over them. Sprinkle with the almonds and dust with icing sugar. Place under the grill for 30–40 seconds or until the sabayon is tinged golden brown. Serve immediately, with crunchy almond biscuits.

STEAMED APRICOT AND ALMOND PUDDING

75g butter, chilled and
   diced, plus extra to
   grease
100g self-raising flour
75g ground almonds
1 tsp baking powder
50g caster sugar
finely grated zest of
   1 lemon
pinch of salt
1 egg
100ml milk

1   Butter a 1 litre pudding basin. Sift the flour, ground almonds and baking powder together into a bowl, then rub in the butter until the mixture resembles breadcrumbs. Stir in the sugar, lemon zest and salt.

2   Lightly beat the egg in a bowl and stir in the milk. Pour this mix slowly into the flour, beating to a smooth batter.

3   For the topping, pour the apricot syrup into a small pan, bring to the boil and bubble to reduce by half.

4   Halve the apricots and lay, cut side up, in the prepared basin. Drizzle the syrup over them, then pour the pudding mixture on top. Cover the pudding basin with greaseproof paper and foil, then secure under the rim with string.

3 apricots in amaretto
   syrup, plus 120ml syrup
   (see page 219)

4 SERVINGS

5   Place a trivet or upturned saucer in a large lidded
heavy-based saucepan. Sit the pudding basin on top and
carefully pour enough boiling water into the pan to come
two-thirds of the way up the sides of the basin. Cover with
the lid and bring to the boil. Steam the pudding for about
1½ hours, checking the water level occasionally and topping
up with boiling water as necessary.

6   Take the pan off the heat and lift out the pudding
basin. Remove the string, foil and paper. Invert a serving
plate on top and, in one swift motion, turn the pudding
basin and plate over to release the pudding on to the plate.
Serve at once, with crème anglaise (see page 251) or cream.

CHERRIES

These are one of summer's real treats. There are literally hundreds of varieties, but they all fall into either the sweet or the sour category. It's all about personal preference, but my favourite kind is the sweet Bigarreau cherries from Céret at the foot of the Pyrenees in France. The plump, dark noir variety and its cousin the tart Bigarreau blanc are both excellent. Of the sour varieties, morello cherries are particularly delicious and produce brilliant dark juices when they are cooked. Of the sweet cherries, soft, juicy Black Tartarian are excellent eaten raw as a dessert fruit.

Before you buy cherries, always take one off the pile and eat it. Some cherries look brilliant and terribly shiny, but taste as acidic as a lemon. Others simply lack flavour. If your fruit tastes sweet and ripe, select a bagful, avoiding any fruit with blemishes or brown stems, and go off and enjoy! Fresh cherries can be kept in a container in the fridge for a few days. Wash them just before eating, otherwise they will absorb water and soften.

Because the homegrown cherry season is so short, I invariably bottle the fruit so we can enjoy it for longer. I use these bottled cherries in all kinds of desserts, including those featured here. I also use cherries in savoury dishes – to accompany roast duckling in particular. Sweet black cherries and hazelnuts go well together, and of course they are divine dipped into a rich chocolate sauce. They are also the traditional fruit in a clafoutis (see page 213), so try my recipe substituting the plums with the best cherries you can find.

POACHED CHERRIES IN BANYULS WINE

600g firm, ripe dark
    cherries (preferably
    Montmorency or Black
    Tartarian), stalks
    removed and washed
75g caster sugar
1 vanilla pod, split
    lengthways
400ml Banyuls wine
    (sweet dessert wine)

4–6 SERVINGS

1   Stone the cherries, keeping them whole. Put the sugar in a saucepan with 100ml water and dissolve over a low heat, then add the vanilla pod and bring to the boil. Simmer for a few minutes to reduce the liquor to a heavy syrup.

2   Meanwhile, in another pan, bring the Banyuls wine to the boil and reduce over a high heat by half. Lower the heat and add the cherries with the sugar syrup. Simmer gently for 8–10 minutes.

3   Ladle the cherries into a warmed sterilised jar, packing them in well and filling the jar almost to the top. Pour the syrup over the fruit. Allow to cool. Seal and store in a cool, dark place for up to 3 months. Refrigerate after opening.

4   Serve with ice cream, or use to enhance other desserts.

PANNA COTTA WITH WARM CHERRIES

2 gelatine leaves
250ml milk
250ml double cream
50g caster sugar
1 vanilla pod, split
½ jar cherries in Banyuls
    wine (see above)

6 SERVINGS

1   Soak the gelatine in cold water to soften. Meanwhile, slowly bring the milk almost to a simmer in a pan. Remove from the heat. Take out the gelatine leaves, squeeze out excess water, then add to the hot milk, stirring to dissolve.

2   In another pan, slowly heat the cream with the sugar and vanilla pod, stirring. As it comes to a simmer, take off the heat, discard the vanilla pod and stir in the milk mix.

3   Pour the mixture into ramekins or dariole moulds and allow to cool, then refrigerate until set.

4   When ready to serve, reheat the cherries in their syrup in a pan over a low heat. Dip the moulds into hot water for a few seconds to release the panna cottas, then turn out on to plates. Arrange the cherries alongside and drizzle some of the syrup over them and the panna cottas. Serve at once.

CHOCOLATE FONDANT WITH CHERRIES AND VANILLA ANGLAISE

The contrast of hot, dark chocolate puddings with melting centres, sweet poached cherries and chilled vanilla anglaise is delightful. Even better, you can prepare everything ahead, ready to pop the puddings into the oven 10 minutes or so before serving.

CHOCOLATE FONDANT

105g dark chocolate (70% cocoa solids), in pieces

105g butter, plus extra for greasing

3 eggs

30g caster sugar

45g plain flour

2 egg yolks

VANILLA ANGLAISE

500ml milk

1 vanilla pod

6 egg yolks

100g caster sugar

TO ASSEMBLE

1 jar cherries in Banyuls wine (see page 225)

4 SERVINGS

1 Butter 4 ramekins or dariole moulds. To make the fondant, melt the chocolate and butter together in a heatproof bowl over a pan of gently simmering water. Meanwhile, beat the whole eggs with the sugar and flour until smoothly blended.

2 When the chocolate has melted, take off the heat and let cool slightly, then beat in the egg yolks, followed by the whisked egg, sugar and flour mix. Pour into the ramekins or darioles. Set aside until ready to bake.

3 For the vanilla anglaise, slowly bring the milk to the boil in a heavy-based pan with the vanilla pod. In the meantime, whisk the egg yolks and sugar together in a bowl using an electric whisk until very pale – almost white. Pour on the hot milk a little at a time, whisking constantly, then pour back into the pan.

4 Stir with a wooden spoon over a low heat for 3 minutes or until the vanilla anglaise has thickened slightly. Do not boil, otherwise it will curdle – the temperature should not exceed 84°C. Pour the sauce into a chilled bowl and allow to cool, then chill.

5 Shortly before serving, preheat the oven to 190°C/Gas 5. Place the ramekins or darioles on a baking sheet and bake in the oven for 12 minutes.

6 Carefully tip the fondants out of their moulds on to serving plates and dust with icing sugar. Surround with the cherries and some of their juice. Spoon the chilled vanilla anglaise around the puddings and serve straight away.

RHUBARB

This is much maligned, perhaps because it has long been regarded as a common, cheap fruit. I, for one, was put off by the endless times it appeared on our school dinner menu in various guises, none of them to be recommended. For years afterwards I couldn't stand the taste of it, but now I have grown to appreciate its fresh flavour and in certain dishes I absolutely love it!

The normal growing season for rhubarb lasts from May to July, but forced rhubarb, grown in hothouses, is available throughout the year. Look out for it especially in spring – its bright pink stems have a fresh flavour and it is more delicate than maincrop rhubarb. Choose firm, crisp rhubarb stalks, store them loosely wrapped in the salad drawer of the fridge and cook within a couple of days.

When cooking, use a minimal amount of liquid and cook for the shortest time possible to maintain the vivid colour. Rhubarb is one fruit that certainly needs sugar to help bring out its flavour, more so with the coarser, greener main crop variety than pink forced rhubarb. Rhubarb is best known for its use in pies, crumbles and jams. You can also use it to make a delicious ice cream, tangy sorbet, creamy fool and a refreshing chilled soup.

I like to fork strands of caramelised rhubarb through a choucroute to serve as an unusual accompaniment to meaty fish. In many recipes, you can use rhubarb as a replacement for other fruits – notably gooseberries. Ginger really enhances the flavour of rhubarb and my rhubarb and ginger crumble is one of my favourite comfort puddings.

RHUBARB AND GINGER CRUMBLE

600g rhubarb, trimmed

2 tsp finely diced
   preserved stem ginger
   in syrup, drained

35g caster sugar

CRUMBLE TOPPING

150g plain flour

125g unsalted butter,
   chilled and diced

165g caster sugar

4–6 SERVINGS

1   Preheat the oven to 200°C/Gas 6. Cut the rhubarb into 3cm pieces, wash well and place in a shallow ovenproof dish with the ginger. Sprinkle with the sugar, toss to mix and set aside.

2   For the crumble topping, put the flour and butter into a food processor and pulse for a few seconds or so until the mixture resembles coarse breadcrumbs. (Don't over-mix otherwise the mixture will form a dough.) Tip into a bowl and stir in the sugar.

3   Scatter the crumble topping evenly over the rhubarb. Bake for about 40–45 minutes until the topping is golden brown and the fruit is tender. Serve with clotted cream or vanilla ice cream.

RHUBARB CREME BRULEE

Try to use the bright pink forced rhubarb for this dessert. Its colour and sharp fruity flavour contrasts beautifully with the smooth vanilla-scented crème brûlée. Crisp dessert biscuits are the perfect complement.

125g rhubarb, trimmed
1 tbsp caster sugar

CUSTARD

3 egg yolks
55g caster sugar
1 vanilla pod, split
   lengthways
1 tbsp milk
230ml double cream

TO SERVE

caster sugar, for dusting

4 SERVINGS

1   Cut the rhubarb into 5cm pieces, wash well and place in a heavy-based pan with the sugar. Cover and cook gently for about 8–10 minutes until tender but still holding its shape. Allow to cool.

2   Meanwhile, make the custard. Put the egg yolks and sugar into a bowl. Scrape out the seeds from the vanilla pod and add to them to the bowl. Whisk to a smooth paste, then whisk in the milk and cream.

3   Divide the rhubarb pieces among four 8cm ramekins, then carefully pour over the custard mix. Refrigerate for an hour before cooking.

4   Preheat the oven to 150°C/Gas 2. Stand the ramekins in a shallow roasting tin and surround with enough boiling water to come halfway up their sides. Cover the surface with a sheet of greaseproof paper and carefully place in the oven. Cook for about 1 hour until just set. Allow to cool, then chill for about an hour.

5   Shortly before serving, sprinkle the crème brûlées generously with caster sugar and caramelise using a cook's blowtorch or under the grill – preheated to its highest setting. Leave to stand for 5 minutes before serving.

STRAWBERRY COMPOTE WITH A RHUBARB GRANITA

STRAWBERRY COMPOTE
400g strawberries, halved
50g caster sugar
2 gelatine leaves

RHUBARB GRANITA
1kg rhubarb, trimmed
250g sugar
juice of 1 lemon
200ml sparkling water

6 SERVINGS

1 For the compote, put the strawberries in a heatproof bowl, sprinkle with the sugar and cover the bowl with cling film. Heat gently in a bain-marie (or over a pan of simmering water) for 10 minutes. Meanwhile, soak the gelatine leaves in cold water to cover to soften.

2 Drain the strawberries in a sieve set over a small pan to catch the juices. Tip the fruit into a bowl and set aside. Simmer the juice over a medium heat to reduce by half. Take off the heat.

3 Squeeze the gelatine to remove excess water, then add to the hot reduced juice, stirring to dissolve. Pour over the strawberries and allow to cool, then cover and chill until ready to serve.

4 To make the granita, wash the rhubarb and cut into 1cm cubes. Place in a glass bowl with the sugar, cover with cling film and microwave on full power for 10 minutes, stirring from time to time. Alternatively, cook gently in a covered heavy-based pan without added liquid for about 10 minutes, stirring occasionally, until soft.

5 Tip the rhubarb into a muslin-lined colander over a bowl and allow the juices to drip through, then squeeze the muslin to extract as much juice and flavour as possible. Discard the residue. Add the lemon juice and sparkling water to the rhubarb juice.

6 Pour the mixture into a shallow freezerproof container and place in the freezer until half-frozen. Remove the partially frozen granita from the freezer and stir with a fork, breaking up the frozen granita. Don't beat it as you would a sorbet – a granita should have the texture of crushed ice. Repeat this process twice more, then freeze until set.

7 To serve, divide the chilled strawberry compote among serving glasses. Spoon the rhubarb granita on top and serve immediately.

RASPBERRIES

These are one of my favourite fruits and I can enjoy them for longer living here in Devon, because the raspberry season seems to start quite early and our summers are longer and finer here in the southwest. Usually we get a second crop of the fruit in September, which is as good as the first in July. Apart from the familiar crimson raspberries, yellow, pink, purple and black varieties are available, though these are rare.

The flavour of raspberries is wonderfully intense. A mere handful mixed with other fruits, such as pears, melon or figs, will make their presence felt. And raspberries make excellent preserves – jams, jellies, flavoured vinegars and eau de vie.

When buying, choose deep-coloured juicy berries that have a beautiful sweet fragrance, avoiding over-ripe fruit. Raspberries are inclined to spoil quickly, so only buy as many as you will consume within a day or two. Alternatively, spread them on a tray and freeze. Once hard, tip into a bag and keep in the freezer until needed. Raspberries freeze more successfully than most other fruits and thereafter lend themselves well to pies, tarts, mousses and soufflés.

Perfect ripe raspberries are, of course, best appreciated on their own or with cream. They also make great ices and sorbets, fillings for sponges and meringues, and a host of other delectable desserts, not least summer pudding. Mix soft, squashy fruit with some sugar, purée in a blender and pass through a sieve, then put a spoonful of this deep red raspberry syrup into a glass, pour over some champagne and enjoy.

RASPBERRY BAVAROIS

3 gelatine leaves
200ml milk
3 eggs, separated
60g caster sugar
600g raspberries,
    carefully washed
250g double cream
icing sugar, to taste

6 SERVINGS

1   Soak the gelatine leaves in a bowl of cold water. Pour the milk into a heavy-based saucepan and slowly bring almost to the boil. Meanwhile, in a bowl, lightly whisk the egg yolks with the sugar. Pour on the hot milk, whisking constantly, then return to the pan.

2   Stir over a low heat with a wooden spoon until the custard slightly thickens (don't let it boil). Immediately remove from the heat and pour through a fine sieve into a large bowl. Squeeze the gelatine leaves to remove excess water, then add them to the hot custard and stir until dissolved. Leave to cool.

3   Set aside a third of the raspberries. Purée the rest in a blender, then pass through a fine sieve into a bowl. Measure 250g of the purée for the bavarois; keep the rest aside.

4   When almost set, pass the custard through a fine sieve into a large bowl. Fold in the 250g raspberry purée. Softly whip the cream and fold into the raspberry custard, then whisk the egg whites to soft peaks and carefully fold in.

5   Pour the mixture into 6 ring moulds, 8cm in diameter and 4cm deep, set on a tray. Chill for about 2 hours to set.

6   Sweeten the reserved raspberry purée with icing sugar to taste. Unmould the bavarois on to plates and top with the reserved berries. Spoon on the raspberry purée to serve.

RASPBERRY SOUFFLE

Soufflés are easier to make than they appear to be. Resist the temptation to open the oven door when they are baking otherwise they might sink, and be ready to serve them straight from the oven. A soufflé should be slightly runny in the centre as you spoon into it.

CREME PATISSIERE

100ml milk

1 vanilla pod

1 egg yolk

50g caster sugar

10g cornflour

10g plain flour

TO COAT THE DISHES

60g unsalted butter, melted

4 tbsp caster sugar

TO ASSEMBLE

60g raspberries

20ml crème de framboise (raspberry liqueur)

1 egg yolk

4 egg whites

60g caster sugar

TO FINISH

icing sugar, for dusting

6 SERVINGS

1   To make the crème pâtissière, pour the milk into a pan, add the vanilla pod and slowly bring to the boil. Meanwhile, whisk the egg yolk and sugar together in a bowl until pale in colour and beginning to thicken. Add the flours and whisk together thoroughly.

2   Pour a third of the hot milk on to the egg mix, whisking until smooth. Pour into the milk in the pan, whisking well. Bring back to the boil, whisking, and cook for 3–4 minutes or until thickened and smooth, whisking constantly. Transfer to a bowl, cover with cling film and set aside to cool.

3   Using a pastry brush, brush 6 deep ramekins, measuring 8cm across and 8cm high with melted butter. Chill to set, then brush with butter again and sprinkle with sugar to coat the inside of the ramekins. Place in the fridge.

4   Preheat the oven to 220°C/Gas 7. Add the raspberries to the crème pâtissière with the liqueur and whisk well until evenly blended. Whisk in the egg yolk and set aside.

5   Using an electric mixer, whisk the egg whites in a clean bowl to soft peaks. Then whisk in the sugar, a spoonful at a time, to make a firm, glossy meringue.

6   Fold half of the egg whites into the pastry cream mixture to lighten it, then very carefully and lightly fold in the rest until fully incorporated.

7   Fill the ramekins with the soufflé mixture to the top and level off with a palette knife, then run your thumb around the edge to clean any spillage. (This also helps the soufflé to rise evenly by not catching on the side.) Stand on a shallow baking tray and bake for 8–10 minutes until the soufflés have risen at least 3cm above the ramekins and are golden brown on top. Dust with icing sugar and serve immediately.

STRAWBERRIES

These epitomise our summers and there are many varieties to choose from. I really don't mind which ones I buy as long as they are fresh, homegrown and taste good. Strawberries first appear as early as May and are with us through the summer. Please don't buy strawberries that originate somewhere in the southern hemisphere in winter. I can assure you that no amount of sugar will improve their flavour. If during the winter months you crave the flavour of strawberries, then enjoy them in their preserved form – as jam, or as a flavoured liqueur or vinegar.

When you are buying them fresh, remember that big strawberries do not necessarily equate to tasty strawberries. More often than not, over-size indicates that they are full of water and likely to lack flavour. Instead, go for strawberries that are bright red, firm and fragrant, with their calyx still intact. If a punnet of strawberries doesn't have a real aroma of the fruit then it is not worth buying.

Strawberries will only retain their quality and flavour for a few days in the fridge and are best eaten soon after buying. If they need washing, do so carefully before you remove the calyx otherwise water will get into the fruit. Ideally, simply wipe with damp kitchen paper.

Strawberries are, of course delicious, just as they are, with or without cream. They also lend themselves to a huge variety of desserts. I like to make a good old-fashioned custard, churn it in my ice-cream maker until it starts to set, then add a load of whole, hulled strawberries, churn for another 5 minutes and serve. It's delicious... try it!

RED FRUIT JELLY

75g sugar

3 lemon tea bags

3¹/₂ gelatine leaves

400g strawberries, hulled

250g blueberries or
blackberries (or a
mixture)

250g raspberries

4–5 SERVINGS

1 Put the sugar in a pan with 500ml water and heat slowly to dissolve the sugar, then bring to the boil. Take off the heat, add the tea bags and leave to infuse for 5 minutes. Meanwhile, soak the gelatine leaves in cold water to soften.

2 Remove the tea bags from the sugar syrup and reheat to just below simmering point. Take off the heat. Squeeze the gelatine leaves to remove excess water, then add to the sugar syrup, stirring to dissolve.

3 Halve or quarter the strawberries and combine with the other fruits. Divide among glass serving bowls to half-fill them. Pour the liquid jelly over the fruit and refrigerate overnight or until the jelly has set.

GRATIN OF STRAWBERRIES

If you can't get hold of lovely sweet strawberries in season, this dessert also works really well with flavourful raspberries.

SABAYON

200g strawberries, hulled
   and halved

50g caster sugar

50ml crème de fraises
   (strawberry liqueur)

3 egg yolks

SPONGE BASES

4 eggs, separated

120g caster sugar

100g plain flour

icing sugar, for dusting

TO ASSEMBLE

50ml crème de fraises
   (strawberry liqueur)

30 small strawberries,
   hulled

6 SERVINGS

1   For the sabayon, place the strawberries in a bowl with the sugar and liqueur. Leave to macerate for at least 3 hours.

2   Meanwhile, make the sponge bases. Preheat the oven to 200°C/Gas 6. In a bowl, whisk the 4 egg yolks and 100g sugar together until pale and fluffy. In another bowl, whisk the egg whites to soft peaks, then gently whisk in the remaining 20g sugar a little at a time. Stir a third of the egg whites into the yolk mix to loosen it, then carefully fold in the rest. Sift in the flour a little at a time and gently fold in.

3   Spoon the sponge mixture into a piping bag fitted with a broad plain nozzle and pipe six 10cm rounds, about 5mm thick on a baking tray lined with greaseproof paper. Dust with a little icing sugar and bake in the oven for 8 minutes. Transfer to a wire rack to cool.

4   Strain the macerated strawberries through a fine sieve over a small pan, pressing with the back of a wooden spoon to extract as much juice as possible. Bring to the boil and let bubble until reduced to 100ml. Allow to cool until tepid.

5   To make the sabayon, whisk the 3 egg yolks and strawberry juice together in a large bowl set over a pan of gently simmering water until the mixture has doubled in volume and is thick enough to leave a ribbon when the beaters are lifted. Remove the bowl from the pan and whisk until the sabayon has cooled a little.

6   Preheat the grill to high. To assemble, dip the sponge discs into the strawberry liqueur to moisten, then place in the centre of 6 heatproof dessert plates. Halve the strawberries and arrange on top. Spoon the sabayon over the strawberries and flash each plate, one at a time, under the grill for a few seconds until the sabayon is tinged golden. Serve immediately.

STRAWBERRY SABLE

This is an impressive dessert. The crisp, melting sablé bases are perfectly contrasted by the creamy vanilla topping and fresh flavourful strawberries. I like to top them with a scoop of strawberry sorbet, but they are almost as good served alone.

500g strawberries, hulled
a little icing sugar, to
    taste

SABLE
80g salted butter
80g caster sugar
2 egg yolks
115g strong plain flour
1 tsp baking powder

VANILLA MOUSSELINE
180g whipping cream
100g pastry cream (see
    page 251)
½ vanilla pod, split

**STRAWBERRY SORBET
(OPTIONAL)**
500g strawberries, hulled
150g caster sugar

4–5 SERVINGS

1   If you are serving the sorbet, make this first. Purée the strawberries in a blender, then pass through a fine sieve into a bowl to remove the seeds. Add the sugar and 50ml water and stir well. Transfer to an ice-cream machine – or sorbetière – and churn until frozen.

2   To prepare the sablé dough, cream the butter and sugar together in a food processor until smooth and very pale (almost white), then mix in the egg yolks. Sift the flour and baking powder together, then add to the mixture and process briefly until just combined.

3   Roll out the sablé dough between two sheets of greaseproof paper to a 5mm thickness, then refrigerate in the paper for 1 hour.

4   Preheat the oven to 180°C/Gas 4. Carefully transfer the sable dough to a baking sheet and bake in the oven for 10–12 minutes or until golden. Leave to stand for a minute or two to firm up a little, then while still hot, cut out 4 or 5 large discs. Set aside.

5   For the vanilla mousseline, whip the cream to soft peaks. Put the pastry cream in another bowl, add the seeds from the vanilla pod and beat until smooth. Fold in the whipped cream and chill until ready to serve.

6   Pureé about 150g of the strawberries in a blender, then pass through a fine sieve into a bowl to make a coulis and sweeten to taste with icing sugar. Cut the rest of the strawberries into neat slices.

7   To assemble, spread some mousseline on each sablé disc and arrange the strawberry slices on top. Drizzle a little coulis over the fruit and around the plate. Top with a scoop of strawberry sorbet if you like.

BASICS

COURT BOUILLON

1 large onion, peeled
1 large carrot, peeled
1 celery stick
1/2 fennel bulb
1 leek, washed
50ml olive oil
60g parsley stalks
2 star anise
1 tsp fennel seeds
1 tsp white peppercorns
50ml white wine vinegar
140ml white wine
1 garlic bulb (unpeeled), cut in half
1 lemon, sliced
30g salt

MAKES ABOUT 2 LITRES

Chop the vegetables. Heat the olive oil in a large pan, add the vegetables and cook gently for about 5 minutes, without colouring. Now add the parsley stalks, star anise, fennel seeds and peppercorns and cook for a further 3 minutes. Add the wine vinegar and reduce until syrupy. Pour in the wine and boil to reduce by half. Now add 2 litres water and bring to the boil. Skim, then lower the heat and simmer for 10 minutes. Add the garlic, lemon slices and salt. The court bouillon is now ready to be used for cooking shellfish, such as crabs and lobsters, or for poaching fish.

CHICKEN STOCK

1.5kg chicken bones
500g chicken wings
3 small carrots, peeled
1 large onion, peeled
1 leek, washed
1 large thyme sprig
1 bay leaf
1 tsp black peppercorns
1/2 garlic bulb, cut in half
salt and pepper

MAKES ABOUT 3 LITRES

Rinse the chicken bones and wings in plenty of cold water, then place in a large saucepan with 4 litres water. Roughly chop the vegetables and add to the pan with the herbs, peppercorns and garlic. Bring to the boil, skim off any scum from the surface, then lower the heat to a gentle simmer. Cook for 2–3 hours then take off the heat, strain and cool. Refrigerate and use within 3 days or freeze for up to 3 months. Season the stock just before using.

FISH STOCK

2kg white fish bones (preferably sole, turbot or halibut)
50ml olive oil
50g unsalted butter
2 onions, peeled and diced
4 garlic cloves, peeled and chopped
1 bay leaf
2 thyme sprigs
2 tarragon sprigs
3 parsley stalks
1/2 tsp fennel seeds
400ml dry white wine
salt and pepper

MAKES ABOUT 1.2 LITRES

Rinse the fish bones in plenty of cold water. Heat the olive oil and butter in a large pan, add the onions and garlic and fry for 5 minutes, without colouring. Add the herbs, fennel seeds and white wine. Turn up the heat and reduce the wine by half. Add the fish bones to the pan, then add about 1.5 litres water to cover. Bring to the boil and skim off the scum from the surface. Lower the heat and simmer gently for 40 minutes, then strain. For a clear stock, strain once more through a muslin-lined sieve. Allow to cool. Refrigerate and use within 2 days or freeze for up to 3 months. Season the stock just before using.

VEGETABLE STOCK

2 onions, peeled
2 large carrots, peeled
3 celery sticks
200g white button mushrooms
2 leeks, washed
2 turnips, peeled
1 swede, peeled
$\frac{1}{2}$ celeriac bulb, peeled
2 flat leaf parsley sprigs
1 small bunch of chervil
1 thyme sprig
1 bay leaf
salt and pepper

MAKES ABOUT 2 LITRES

Chop the vegetables, place in a large saucepan and cover with 2 litres water. Add the herbs, season and bring to the boil. Lower the heat, cover and simmer gently for 30 minutes. Tip into a bowl and let cool. Strain the cooled stock through a colander, then through a muslin-lined sieve to trap any sediment. Refrigerate and use within 5 days or freeze for up to 3 months. Check the seasoning before using.

MEAT GLAZE

2kg beef or veal bones
2 pigs trotters, washed
1 large onion, peeled
1 leek, washed
2 celery sticks, washed
2 carrots
5 garlic cloves, peeled
1 bay leaf
3 thyme sprigs
1 tsp black peppercorns

MAKES ABOUT 200ML

Preheat the oven to 200°C/Gas 6. Put the bones in a roasting tray and roast in the oven for 45 minutes or until well browned. Chop the pigs trotters, quarter the onion and chop the other vegetables. Put all the ingredients, including the bones into a large pan and cover with water. Bring to the boil, skim, then lower the heat and simmer for at least 4 hours. Strain the stock through a colander, then once again through a fine sieve. Cool and refrigerate overnight.

The next day, remove any fat from the surface. Bring the stock to the boil and reduce by half, then pass through a muslin-lined sieve into a clean pan. Boil to reduce down until thick enough to coat the back of a spoon, lowering the heat as the glaze thickens so it doesn't burn. Pour the meat glaze into a container and refrigerate. Or freeze in ice-cube trays. Use to add a real depth of flavour to gravy, etc.

BRAISED TOMATO SAUCE

1kg ripe plum tomatoes
90ml olive oil
1 carrot, peeled and diced
2 celery stalks, diced
1 large onion, peeled and chopped
1 tsp white peppercorns, crushed
1 bay leaf
1 thyme sprig
60g tomato purée
30g caster sugar
90ml white wine vinegar
120ml white wine
2 garlic cloves, peeled and crushed
1 basil sprig
handful of parsley stalks
300ml chicken stock (see page 247)
salt, to taste

MAKES ABOUT 150ML

Halve, deseed and dice the tomatoes; set aside. Heat the olive oil in a deep saucepan, add the carrot, celery and onion and fry until golden. Add the pepper, bay leaf, thyme and tomato purée and cook, stirring, for 3–4 minutes. In another pan, dissolve the sugar in the vinegar and boil to reduce down to a light syrup. Add the wine to the vegetables and let bubble to reduce by half. Add the garlic, basil, parsley and stock, then the syrupy mix and tomatoes. Bring to the boil, lower the heat and gently simmer for about 1 hour, skimming and stirring occasionally. Pass the sauce through a fine sieve, season and reheat to serve.

HOLLANDAISE SAUCE

25g unsalted butter
1 shallot, peeled and finely chopped
1 garlic clove, peeled and finely chopped
1/2 tsp white peppercorns, crushed
1 thyme sprig
1 tarragon sprig
1/2 bay leaf
1 parsley stalk
25ml white wine vinegar
25ml dry white wine
2 egg yolks
75ml warm clarified butter (see page 251)
salt and cayenne pepper
juice of 1/2 lemon

SERVES 4

Melt the butter in a small pan and add the shallot, garlic, crushed pepper and herbs. Cook for 5 minutes, without colouring. Add the wine vinegar and boil until totally reduced, then add the wine and reduce until syrupy. Strain and set aside.
Whisk the egg yolks with 1 1/2 tsp water in a heatproof bowl set over a pan of barely simmering water until thick. Slowly whisk in the clarified butter, then add the wine and shallot reduction, whisking to a smooth, thick sauce. Season with a little salt and cayenne and add the lemon juice, to taste. Serve warm, as soon as possible; do not reheat.

BUTTER SAUCE

2 shallots or 1 onion, finely chopped
1 garlic clove, peeled and chopped
1 thyme sprig
1 tarragon sprig
1/2 bay leaf
1/2 tsp white peppercorns, crushed
250g unsalted butter, diced
2 tbsp white wine vinegar
2 tbsp white wine
2 tbsp double cream
salt
squeeze of lemon juice

MAKES 300ML

Put the shallots, garlic, herbs and crushed pepper in a small saucepan with 20g of the butter and heat gently, stirring, until the butter has melted. Add the wine vinegar and boil to reduce until syrupy. Add the wine and reduce again until syrupy. Pour in the cream and, as soon as it boils, lower the heat. Add the butter, piece by piece, stirring constantly until it is all melted and you have a smooth sauce. Season with salt and add a little lemon juice to taste. Pour the sauce through a fine sieve into another small pan and keep warm until ready to serve.

Chervil (or chive) butter sauce
Stir 4 tbsp chopped chervil (or chives) into the finished sauce.

HERB AND ANCHOVY BUTTER

250g unsalted butter, diced
2 shallots, peeled and diced
2 garlic cloves, peeled and diced
2 tbsp white wine
1 thyme sprig, leaves only, finely chopped
1/2 bay leaf, finely chopped
30g chopped parsley
1 tsp chopped capers
3 gherkins, finely chopped
2 anchovy fillets, chopped
6 tarragon leaves, blanched and chopped
2 egg yolks
juice of 1/2 lemon

MAKES 300G

Melt 20g of the butter in a small pan and cook the shallots and garlic until soft and translucent. Add the wine and reduce by half, then add the chopped thyme and bay leaf and cook for a further 1 minute. Allow to cool.
Put the rest of the butter into a food processor and whiz until it turns white and fluffy. Add the parsley, capers, gherkins, anchovies, tarragon, egg yolks and lemon juice. Whiz briefly to mix, then add the shallot mixture and combine.
Place the butter on a sheet of greaseproof paper, roll up into a sausage and refrigerate until needed.

TARRAGON VINAIGRETTE

juice of $\frac{1}{2}$ lemon
120ml white wine vinegar
salt and pepper
pinch of caster sugar
500ml olive oil
2 garlic cloves, peeled and halved
3 tarragon sprigs

MAKES 650ML

Put the lemon juice, wine vinegar, salt, pepper and sugar in a bowl. Whisk in the olive oil, then, using a small funnel, pour into a jar or bottle, and add the garlic cloves and tarragon. Put a lid or cork on the bottle or jar and allow to infuse for at least an hour. Shake well before using. This dressing will keep in the fridge for a week.

Fish vinaigrette
Heat 100ml fish stock (see page 247) and reduce by two-thirds. Allow to cool slightly, then mix with 100ml tarragon vinaigrette.

HAZELNUT VINAIGRETTE

1 tbsp sherry vinegar
1 tsp lemon juice
150ml groundnut oil
150ml hazelnut oil
1 small garlic clove, peeled and crushed
pinch of caster sugar
salt and pepper

MAKES 300ML

Whisk the ingredients together in a bowl until evenly combined. Pour through a funnel into a small bottle or jar and seal with a cork or airtight lid. Shake the vinaigrette well before using. This dressing will keep in the fridge for a couple of weeks.

Walnut vinaigrette
Use walnut oil in place of hazelnut oil.

MAYONNAISE

2 large egg yolks
1 tsp Dijon mustard
$\frac{1}{2}$ tsp salt
200ml sunflower oil
100ml olive oil
2 tbsp white wine vinegar
white pepper
lemon juice, to taste

MAKES ABOUT 300ML

Put the egg yolks, mustard and salt in a bowl and whisk together. Mix the oils together in a jug, then slowly whisk into the yolk mixture, a few drops at a time to begin with, then in a steady stream. When half of the oil is incorporated, add the wine vinegar. Continue to whisk in the remaining oil to make a thick, glossy mayonnaise. Check the seasoning and add a squeeze of lemon juice to taste.

Note To save time, you can make the mayonnaise in a food processor, adding the oil to the base mix through the funnel while the motor is running.

Herb mayonnaise
Finely chop 3 tbsp chervil, chives or parsley (or a mixture) and stir into the mayonnaise at the end.

Tarragon mayonnaise
Blanch the leaves from 3 tarragon sprigs in boiling water for 10 seconds, refresh in iced water, drain and pat dry with kitchen paper, then chop very finely. Make the mayonnaise as above, adding the tarragon at the end.

Garlic (and tarragon) mayonnaise
Omit the mustard. Add 2 crushed garlic cloves at the beginning with the egg yolks. Add 3 blanched tarragon sprigs (as for tarragon mayonnaise) as well if you like.

CLARIFIED BUTTER

350g unsalted butter, cut into small pieces

MAKES 200ML

Melt the butter in a small saucepan over a gentle heat. As the butter melts, the whey and impurities will rise to the surface. Using a ladle, skim these off and discard. There will be some 'milk' below the melted butter. Carefully pour the clarified butter into a bowl through a sieve lined with muslin to trap all the impurities. Stop pouring when you reach the milk. Use the clarified butter as required.

PASTRY CREAM

600ml milk
1 vanilla pod, split
6 egg yolks
120g caster sugar
25g cornflour
30g plain flour

MAKES 800G

Pour the milk into a pan and scrape in the seeds from the vanilla pod. Add the empty pod to the milk as well and slowly bring to the boil. Meanwhile, whisk the egg yolks and sugar together in a bowl until pale in colour and beginning to thicken. Sift in the flours and whisk together thoroughly. Remove the vanilla pod, then pour a third of the hot milk over the egg mix, whisking until smooth. Pour into the milk in the pan, whisking well. Bring back to the boil, whisking, and cook for 3–4 minutes or until thickened and smooth, whisking constantly. Transfer to a bowl, cover with cling film and set aside to cool. Refrigerate until ready to use.

CREME ANGLAISE

500ml milk
1 vanilla pod, split
6 egg yolks
100g caster sugar
200ml double cream

SERVES 6–8

Pour the milk into a pan and scrape in the seeds from the vanilla pod. Add the empty pod to the milk as well and slowly bring to the boil. Whisk the egg yolks and sugar together in a bowl until pale. Remove the vanilla pod from the hot milk, then pour half of it over the yolks, whisking all the time. Pour the mixture back into the milk in the pan, whisking well. Return to a medium-low heat and stir constantly until the custard has thickened enough to coat the back of a wooden spoon. Do not boil, or the custard will curdle. Strain through a fine sieve into a bowl and whisk in the cream.

SHORTCRUST PASTRY

375g plain flour
1 tsp salt
225g unsalted butter, diced
1 egg, lightly beaten

MAKES '375G QUANTITY'

Sift the flour and salt into a bowl, add the butter and rub it into the flour until the mixture resembles coarse breadcrumbs. Make a well in the centre and add the beaten egg with enough cold water (about 3–4 tbsp) to bind everything together. Mix gently until smooth, then press into a ball, wrap the pastry in cling film and refrigerate for 30 minutes before rolling out.

INDEX

Special thanks to my chefs Robert Spencer, Nigel Marriage, Robin Zavou, Julien Picamil, James Barber, Colin Leggett and Andreas Karatzas for their input; to my PA Rachael Birss for all her hard work and typing skills; to Bo and Elaine Steer at Creative Talent Ltd; to my local suppliers, in particular Bob Ward at AW Luscombe (butcher), Nick Henry at Moby Nicks (fishmonger) and Paul Evans (Wilton Farm Produce); David Loftus for his brilliant photography; Royal Doulton, All-cladd and Churchill China for the loan of props; and to Anne Furniss, Janet Illsley and Vanessa Courtier, and all at Quadrille.